BFI Modern Classics

Rob White
Series Editor

BFI Modern Classics is a series of critical studies of films produced over the last three decades. Writers explore their chosen films, offering a range of perspectives on the dominant art and entertainment medium in contemporary culture. The series gathers together snapshots of our passion for and understanding of recent movies.

Also Published

The Matrix
Joshua Clover

(see a full list of titles in the series at the back of this book)

The Thin Red Line

Michel Chion

Translated by
Trista Selous

 Publishing

First published in 2004 by the
British Film Institute
21 Stephen Street, London W1T 1LN

The British Film Institute promotes greater
understanding and appreciation of,
and access to, film and moving image
culture in the UK.

Series design by Andrew Barron
& Collis Clements Associates

Typeset in Italian Garamond
and Swiss 721BT by
D R Bungay Associates,
Burghfield, Berks

Printed in the UK by
Norwich Colour Print, Drayton, Norfolk

British Library Cataloguing-in-Publication Data
A catalogue record for this book is available
from the British Library

ISBN 1-84457-044-4

Contents

Acknowledgments

I should very much like to thank Rob White, for having had the idea for this book and commissioning me to write it.

I should also like to thank Kazuko Nii, who translated the Japanese dialogue for me. As always, my discussions with my wife Anne-Marie have been invaluable and I am also grateful to Carlo Hintermann, Gustavo Costantini and Michel Ciment for their encouragement.

The Thin Red Line

'Why are we **born into the world** and **part of the world**, while at the same time feeling that we have been exiled from it?

Why doesn't the world's **haunting beauty** prevent us from being alone and suffering?

What is **language**, which allows different people's voices to ask each other the same questions, and makes many voices into the single voice of the person questioning the world, while at the same time, at the moment of death, this same language erects **absolute barriers** between people, simply because one speaks American and the other Japanese?

Why are human beings, friends and enemies, separated from each other, while at the same time so clearly being reflections for each other, being so clearly the same spark of consciousness and language, capable of **walking through the garden of the world** and wondering?

Terrence Malick's three films to date, particularly the one under consideration in this book, are interrogatory works, whose role is to **make questions resonate in the universe**, and speech in the world.

While the questions are posed as directly as possible, the link the director weaves between these questions and the geographical, historical, human and fleshly realities he describes is far more enigmatic, complex and ambiguous.

A memory of Witt's childhood: born in the world and part of the world

Badlands, *Days of Heaven* and *The Thin Red Line* all seem to speak of an "earthly paradise" that is at once lost and ever-present. All three allow one or several of their characters to be not just a finite body in space and a psychologically defined character but also an inner (or narrative) voice, a strange voice that speaks outside space, giving these characters **a different, more general personality, located between themselves and all other human beings**. Theirs is a voice detached from the women (the female voices of *Badlands* and *Days of Heaven*) and men (the various male voices of *The Thin Red Line*) of the films. It is a voice that bursts the bounds of the "**moving box**" – the phrase used in *The Thin Red Line* – that is the brain, the mind of every human being, which carries other people within it, but is separate from them, which carries within it the beauty of the world and of other people, but is separate from them.'

I sent the above to Rob White when this book was still no more than a project. In writing it I was gradually overcome by the embarrassing sense of having nothing more to say, of having already encompassed all the thoughts inspired in me by this sublime film, which I could happily sit and admire in childlike silence.

But let's go on anyway, let's explore the details.

A good place to start is with the title, taken from James Jones's novel, *The Thin Red Line* (1962). Although the words officially refer to the line between life and death, they surely also speak to us of barriers and limits, those mysterious limits that we sense everywhere around us and do not know how to cross. In this film, voices are continually asking questions that it is not our role to answer, but which must be listened to and allowed to resonate.

At the end of the film, one of the characters – the man who has asked himself the most questions, Witt (Jim Caviezel) – has given his life for the others, and another character – a survivor this time, Welsh (Sean Penn) – is walking through the world with the sense that he is enclosed in a 'moving box'. But perhaps Welsh has rediscovered that spark of consciousness and anxiety that had been extinguished within him. Perhaps the death of an individual is what allows the flame to move from one to another.

At the end of the film, echoing in response to the many questions, come not answers but three pleas – or prayers.

The plea (by letter) of a woman to her absent husband, who has gone to war and whom she wants to leave: 'Help me leave you.'

The plea of the living man, Welsh, walled up in himself as though dead, who wants to be able to feel the lack again: 'Let me feel the lack.' This is a plea with no precise addressee.

The last plea, carried by the voice of a dead man – Witt – speaking from the place of an immortality unknown to us, and addressed not to God but to his own soul: 'O my Soul, let me be in you now.' It is also a prayer for his soul to be in him, to see: 'Look out through my eyes, look out at the things you made, all things shining.'

'All things', from the highest mountain to the humblest leaf, brought together and made equal by Malick's cinema.

Cinema is the art that makes it possible to place the large and small things of this world on the same scale, making them figure at the same size in the changeless frame of the screen. In Terrence Malick's cinema, the animal living its animal life, the landscape and the sun, human beings, their questions, their preoccupations and their machines are all placed on the same scale. The film uses its own means (framing, editing, sound, light) to illuminate the strange cohabitation of human beings with animals and with the world, in the same 'moving box'.

This cohabitation is also, as we shall see, a lack of 'communication'.

The Unanswered Question

Around 1 hour 47 minutes and 20 seconds after *The Thin Red Line* begins, in the background and directly following an element from the original score written by Hans Zimmer, the audience hears a short extract from a work by the American composer Charles Ives (1874–1954), *The Unanswered Question*. This musical quotation, which ends three minutes later, is laid over the sounds and images of 'dialogue' (if that term is applicable, as each character is speaking his own language) between a dying Japanese prisoner and an American soldier whom we might regard as cruel, since he is making a collection of his enemies' teeth.

We shall come back to this scene, and what the characters are saying 'to each other'.

This short piece of music (six to seven minutes, depending on the tempo at which it is played), composed in 1906, was intended by Ives to form part of a diptych with another aural tableau, *Central Park in the Dark*, a 'contemplation' for full orchestra written in the same year. But while the composer regarded the latter work – an evocation of twilight in the famous Manhattan park, firmly anchored in the tradition of descriptive music – as the 'contemplation of Nothing Serious', *The Unanswered Question* was intended to be the 'contemplation of a serious matter', a 'cosmic landscape', a directly metaphysical work, with no narrative support.

In it the 'eternal question of existence' is posed by a short theme on the trumpet (a part that Ives indicated could equally be played on the oboe, cor anglais or clarinet) over a 'background' of sustained, perfect chords on the strings, representing the 'silence of the Druids, who know, see and hear nothing'. The question posed by the trumpet receives unsatisfactory, unsynchronised answers, or attempts at answers (in a part of the work that Malick did not use), in the form of chromatic motifs played on two flutes, an oboe and a clarinet.

In 1906, and with very simple means, Charles Ives's symphonic poem managed to propose an entirely new kind of music, with no rhythmic pulsation, a predominance of sustained notes and a form without symmetry. Above all, the three layers of the questioning instrument, the small group of instruments giving evasive answers and the mass of strings providing the background are all harmonically, rhythmically and in other ways independent. Rather than 'poly-tonality', this might better be termed 'poly-music', freely combining heterogeneous, independent elements, which are played in combination with each other, but remain in their separate worlds.

While in *Central Park in the Dark*, the 'background' was atonal and the 'figure' diatonic, here it is the other way round. In *The Unanswered Question*, the background is tonal while the thematic figures are not. The 'background' of *Central Park* evokes the darkness of the coming night,

A Melanesian man passes by American soldiers

while in *The Unanswered Question* it evokes both silence and deafness. The more serene part of the music seems 'deaf' to the trumpet solo poured out into space, like a solitary voice to which no one is listening.

Similarly, in *The Thin Red Line*, voices speak but, on the pretext that they are 'inner', no one on screen hears them. There are animals that no one looks at but are present nonetheless. There is also a Melanesian man who passes some American soldiers, but walks on as if he has neither seen nor heard them.

In trying to describe Ives's music, the words 'background' and 'figure' spring inevitably to mind; one cannot avoid thinking of them – yet at the same time, they seem inadequate. When background and figure pay no attention to each other, which is figure and which is background? Malick's cinema asks us the same kind of question: what is background (the set, the setting) and what figure (who is its principal character – is there one even, since they often change; what is the subject)? It is not enough to say, background and figure are one and the same. The question remains present and inescapable.

It is striking that the section of *The Thin Red Line* that quotes the Charles Ives piece – which seems largely to have inspired the aesthetics of part of Hans Zimmer's score – begins with the words, 'What is this war?' and continues with 'Why?', 'Who's doing this?', 'Are you here?' and 'Where does it come from?'. No signs are given suggesting that these questions have even been heard. In contrast to Tarkovsky's world, in which nature is also very present, with Malick nothing in nature ever gives any sign to human beings.

These questions are not only posed verbally by the soldiers in erratic, fragmented interior monologues, they are also embodied in the mysterious relationships created by the way shots are cut together, in the contrast between small details and big events, between the sunlight passing through the holes in the leaf of a tree and the death of a wounded youth.

Like Charles Ives's music, Malick's film places diverse elements side by side, without seeking to answer the question posed by their juxtaposition.

In linguistics, the juxtaposition of different elements, without the use of terms to create a temporal, causal or logical relationship between them, is known as *parataxis*, while *hypotaxis* is its opposite, in other words the establishment of a relationship between different elements linked by an explicit relationship such as causality or subordination. A quantity of contemporary literature and cinema both uses and abuses parataxis: there is this, and at the same time – or then – there is that, and it's up to the viewer who feels so inclined to create a relationship between them. What is called 'modernism' (for example in Godard's work) makes great use of this approach. Terrence Malick's films also use parataxis, but in a highly personal way and not, as is too often the case, by applying it mechanically.

I shall try to talk about this film without claiming to answer the questions it embodies – for example, with a ready-made spiritualist or Christian response, as some French critics have done.

It so happens that Charles Ives was a great admirer of the American writers and poets sometimes called the 'transcendentalists', notably Ralph Waldo Emerson (1803–82) and Henry David Thoreau (1817–62), author of *Walden*. Indeed, he dedicated a very long piano sonata, the *Concord Sonata*, to them, named after the Massachusetts town where these writers lived.

Malick's work is frequently linked to the names of Thoreau, Emerson and also the poet Walt Whitman, due to the strong presence of nature in his films and an associated spirituality that first becomes clearly apparent in *Days of Heaven* (1978).

Badlands (1973), Malick's first film, takes its title from the name of a region in the United States. The film, based on a real news item, tells the strange story of a killer on the run with his young girlfriend, transporting us into different, sometimes very wild settings, and ending in a small aeroplane, into which a handcuffed Martin Sheen has been placed, surrounded by a sea of clouds to which he pays very little attention. The humour of the film stems from the fact that the character reads *National Geographic*, but seems to remain indifferent to the nature around him. *Days of Heaven*, shot in Alberta, Canada, but whose action is set on a Texas farmstead, unfolds almost entirely in the open air. The characters

are almost never seen with a roof over their heads, although the film begins and ends in Chicago. Here again, the characters never admire the sunset or the beauty of the fields and cloudy sky; after all, this is their workplace. They speak only of themselves and their lives. Rich in vast landscapes and luxuriant vegetation, *The Thin Red Line* begins and ends with water: a marsh and a lagoon. In the memories of some characters, we see not cities but fields, or the Pacific shoreline, or the familiar walls of a bedroom, which seems to have no ceiling and to be open to the sky (related to the abandoned, ruined house of the colonial plantation where Welsh and Witt have their last conversation, shortly before the latter's death).

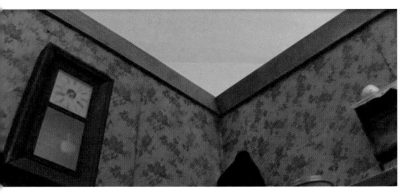

Sunlight through a broken leaf: the last vision of a dying man. A bedroom which seems to be open to the sky

I have never read any interview with Malick, or any accounts from those who have worked with him, that establishes a knowledge of and like for Thoreau, Emerson or Whitman. But it is hard not to think of them.

Birth of a Legend

As we know, in thirty years Malick has made only three features, none of which has had immense commercial success, but all of which have been noticed and admired. After *The Thin Red Line*, he worked on a project on the life of the revolutionary Che Guevara (due to be played by Benicio del Toro, who co-wrote the script), but early in 2004 it was announced that he would first shoot *The New World*, a film based on the landing of British colonisers on the Amerindian coastline in the 18th century, with Colin Farrell in the leading role. This unconventional career, and the fact that Malick gives few interviews and rarely agrees to be photographed, has contributed to the legend that has built up around him.

Born in Waco, Texas, on 30 November 1943, Malick grew up in Austin (where he studied at the Episcopalian school) and Oklahoma. His father worked for Philips Petroleum. According to Michel Ciment, during the summer Terrence worked in the oil wells and went north for the harvest, sleeping on Greyhound buses and hanging around with the tramps and seasonal workers. At high school he played American football; he went to Harvard in 1961. There he was taught by Stanley Cavell, author of the famous essay on American cinema, *The Pursuit of Happiness*. He read Ludwig Wittgenstein (whose investigations into language seem to have left their mark on him) and Martin Heidegger, did not finish his thesis and worked in London as a journalist for *Newsweek*.

In an interview from 1974 with the French magazine *Positif*, Malick described how, 'As children, we were trained in exercises of passive defence against a nuclear attack. At the time we used to get under the desks. People were building shelters.'[1] The fear of nuclear weapons in the 1950s, directly evoked in *Badlands*, is often little understood or forgotten in today's descriptions of that period. It seems to have been particularly developed in two countries: Japan of course, theatre of the first atomic bombardments, but also the very country whose leaders had taken it upon themselves to unleash such a terrifying weapon, the United States. Leaving aside the many science-fiction films based on the risk of nuclear apocalypse (Robert Wise's *The Day the Earth Stood Still*, 1951; Stanley Kramer's *On the Beach*, 1959) or the monstrous mutations created by radioactivity (Gordon Douglas's *Them!*, 1954; Robert Wise's *The Incredible Shrinking Man*, 1957), even some detective films such as Robert Aldrich's masterpiece *Kiss Me Deadly* (1955) are haunted by this danger. Although none of Malick's films deals directly with the bomb, they are all bathed in an atmosphere of threat and constant danger, including *Days of Heaven*, ostensibly a social melodrama set in the 1910s (in which the young female narrator speaks of hellfire and the end of the world).

Malick also reveals, 'I was raised in an atmosphere of violence in Texas. And what struck me was that violence would burst out and be over before anyone really had time to realise.' This is exactly what happens in his first two films: violence is at once very present (particularly in the first) and unreal, both because it is hardly or never mentioned and because the director avoids any overly explicit display of its effects on bodies, such as corpses, the impact of bullets, blood flowing or wounds. While retaining the same visual restraint in the representation of the mutilated human body,[2] *The Thin Red Line* spends a very long time preparing the viewer and characters for their meeting with violence and murder, in the ritualised, demented context in which it is authorised by society – in other words war.

Malick won a scholarship to Oxford, but dropped out a year later and became a journalist with the *New Yorker.* He spent four months in Bolivia with the intention of writing about Che Guevara and the trial of the French revolutionary Regis Debray, but published nothing.

He then went back to the United States and taught philosophy at Massachusetts Institute of Technology for a year. In 1969 he decided to give up teaching and applied to study at the American Film Institute. Two years later he began work on his first feature, *Badlands*, released in 1973.

At the AFI he made a short called *Lanton Mills*, featuring Harry Dean Stanton, Warren Oates and himself: two cowboys leave the West on horseback, enter the modern world and try to rob a bank. We should note that none of Malick's feature-length films, made or unmade, is set in the contemporary period; all are located in a close or distant past. At the same time, he was making a reputation for himself as a script doctor. In particular, he mentions working on an early version of *Dirty Harry*, to be directed by Irving Kershner and starring Marlon Brando. Siegel eventually made the film in 1971, with a different screenplay and Clint Eastwood, launching a series featuring the same character as well as a whole current of 'dirty cop movies'.

The screenplay of *Badlands* was based on a true story of teenage murderers on the run, dating from the 1950s, whose source Malick promised not to reveal out of respect for people still living. His idea was to use the girl's narrative voiceover to show that she does not live in the same world as the hero. From the outset, the director was thinking about the counterpoint between voiceover and images, which was instantly remarked on and has been a constant feature of his films:

I wanted Holly to talk like a fourteen-year-old girl who wants to make the best possible impression … The commentary 'off' was crucial. It made possible the humour that arises from the mistaken idea she has of the audience. She doesn't really know who she's talking to. When she goes across the Badlands she thinks what we want to know isn't what's happening between Kit and herself, but what they ate on the journey.

Instead of showing a couple who are on the same wavelength, the film stresses the difference in age and attitudes between the two protagonists: 'I thought that it would be one of the ironies of the film that even a series of murders couldn't affect a girl like that, that she would always have her feet on the ground, she wouldn't be caught out.'

Badlands was shot in Colorado, the Dust Bowl and South Dakota. Part of it was carefully scripted, the rest (the scenes in the forest) largely improvised. This was not apparent to the critics, some of whom found the film too 'preconceived' (this impression disappeared with the following film). It was hailed by Jonathan Rosenbaum as 'one of the finest examples of narrated cinema since the early days of Welles and Abraham Polonsky' and, without box-office success, established

Malick's reputation with the critics, the film world and a section of the public.

The film creates a continual sense of unease in the viewer, since the main character carries out his various murders in a cold, almost calm way, while the music, voiceover and bucolic or forest settings cloak the whole in an air of unreality. This might seem the opposite of what happens in *The Thin Red Line*, which is by contrast a very expansive film, emotional, warm and full of feeling.

In 1974 Malick said of *Badlands*, 'I was very concerned at the idea that my film might be seen as lacking in heart, because I'm an admirer of Kazan, Stevens and Penn, I love big emotional scenes.' However, he goes on, 'I wanted to keep a distance from my characters, that's why I rejected hand-held camera movements.' We shall see how far *The Thin Red Line* manages curiously to maintain such a distance, while getting much closer to faces and bodies and with a great many camera movements.

The director had already shown his interest in social reality in choosing Martin Sheen (real name Ramon Estevez) as his leading actor, who – as he himself says – really did come from a very humble background. Similarly the heroes of the second and third features would be people from lowly origins.

In his second feature, *Days of Heaven*, which had a bigger budget, at one point the characters watch an extract from *The Immigrant* (1917), which makes us think that Malick had watched not only Chaplin but also Kazan's *America America* (1963): emotion, universalism and exile.

Days of Heaven, shot in 1978, is set in Texas at the beginning of World War I. Leaving aside the fact that it was one of the first films to make the subtle sounds of nature audible through the successful use of Dolby, it is a very curious, haunting work, which places the audience in an unstable position while simultaneously enchanting them. The main story, a classic love-triangle (Abby, Bill, the farmer), is treated in a repetitive, confused and distant way, without generating any interest in the feelings of Abby or Bill. On the other hand, every time the character of the little girl – the extraordinary Linda Manz – or the local people – workers, farmhands and priests – appear, the film becomes more expansive.

Days of Heaven was not a great commercial success and for twenty years no new film by Malick was released, despite various projects that never came to fruition (including one on the life of John Merrick, the elephant man, before the film directed by David Lynch and produced by Mel Brooks). It took two brave and tenacious producers to enable Malick to make one of two projects they took on. These were Molière's *Tartuffe* and the film that was finally made, *The Thin Red Line*.

Jones's story, to whose plot Malick made profound changes in his screenplay – softening the violence, leaving aside themes of racism and homophobia, tempering the harsh climate of the setting, which plays a major role in the novel, and also having the character of Witt die – is set during the Pacific War and the battle of Guadalcanal.

Guadalcanal, one of the Solomon Islands conquered by the Japanese and retaken by the Americans in 1942–3, has been the subject of many films, including one with the same title as Malick's and based on the same novel, *The Thin Red Line* (1964), directed by Andrew Marton, in CinemaScope and black and white, with Keir Dullea (later the lead in Kubrick's *2001*, 1968) and Jack Warden. We should note that this was an average production, with no stars. Others on the same theme, and closer to the actual events, are Lewis Seiler's *Guadalcanal Diary* (1943), with Preston Foster, Lloyd Nolan, William Bendix and Anthony Quinn, and Nicholas Ray's *Flying Leathernecks* (1951), a film said to be violent, in

Jim Caviezel as Witt

which two naval officers, played by John Wayne and Robert Ryan, fight the Japanese and clash with each other.

The budget for *The Thin Red Line* was over $50 million and the film was shot near Port Douglas in northern Australia in 1997, a location considered quite similar to the historical setting of the action. Certain scenes were shot on Guadalcanal itself and in San Pedro, California.

The film has a large cast. A number of stars agreed to lend their faces and reputations to sometimes minor roles out of admiration for Malick.

There is a surprising contrast between the names and faces featured on the film poster and the film itself. John Travolta and George Clooney (already stars when the film was released) figure in the main credits, yet both make only very brief appearances, reduced almost to nothing in the case of Clooney's character (he plays Bosche, Staros's replacement, for less than a minute). Other well-known stars, such as Nick Nolte and Sean Penn, have major roles, but Woody Harrelson (famous since Oliver Stone's *Natural Born Killers*, 1994) dies a third of the way through the film. By contrast, Jim Caviezel as Witt, who, though not spending much time on screen, gives the story its thread, was not yet the star he has become since Mel Gibson's *The Passion of the Christ* (2004). Elias Koteas, who gives a remarkable performance as Staros, has remained little-known as an actor.

As a result, this is not so much an anti-star film, peopled only by anonymous faces, as a film that places itself beyond the difference between primary and secondary roles or between famous actors and others who are unknown or little-known. For the viewer this has a disturbing effect of mixing up identities and making roles relatively interchangeable, reinforced by the fact that some soldiers' names are mentioned seldom or not at all in the dialogue. I was able to identify Doll, played by Dash Mihok – a fair-haired young man whose eyes and mouth are constantly open wide with fear – only because I had noticed his performance in Baz Luhrmann's film of *Romeo + Juliet* (1996), in which he played the secondary role of Benvolio. Furthermore, in the editing Malick continually cuts between all the characters, making it hard to put names to either characters or actors.

This is not a film of anti-heroes, it is a film in which the function of hero is a baton that is passed around.

A Story of Redemption?

Though *The Thin Red Line* is split into a great many scenes, which are themselves sometimes fragmented or interrupted by often brief flashbacks, its construction nevertheless remains fairly clear, if asymmetrical. I shall describe its main outlines, referring to the more detailed synopsis supplied as an appendix.

1. Witt AWOL: a short, but important section of the film shows us an American soldier who has gone AWOL from his company, and is caught. There is an initial 'dialogue' between Witt and Welsh: the former has 'seen another world', a Melanesian earthly paradise, and the second believes that there is only one world, that it's a hard one and a man must let nothing touch him.

2. A second, slightly longer section on a ship off the Solomon Islands, with Lieutenant Colonel Tall (Nick Nolte) and Brigadier General Quintard (John Travolta), acts as an introductory scene. Quintard outlines the aim of the coming battle, which is to dislodge the Japanese from the island, where they have established themselves and built an airport. Guadalcanal controls access to Japan and also gives the Japanese access to the Allies. According to the general, and to the lieutenant colonel when he passes the orders on to those under his command, it is important that it should be captured: 'Guadalcanal could be the turning point in the war',

The beauty of a tree at the start of the film

Tall says to Staros. For Tall, it may also be the turning point in his career. He is getting older and has not been promoted (the film does not tell us whether or not he receives his promotion later; unlike many historical films, it abstains from any final recapitulation and abandons many characters along the way, including Tall).

According to some historians, the battle of Guadalcanal had little strategic importance in the real course of events – but this is easier to say with hindsight. What matters here is that the film deliberately gives us no assessment, whether through image, dialogue, voiceover or a final rolling title, of the historical impact of the battle or of the importance later accorded to the events for the course of World War II. In watching the film, we, like the characters, are plunged into the events in the present; we do not know in advance what is important and what is not.

Through what the soldiers say we also get to know C Company, to which most of the characters we shall see belong. It is led by Captain Staros, of Greek origin, with First Sergeant Welsh as second-in-command.

When the soldiers land, they are terrified of being bombed by the Japanese; this doesn't happen.

3. A very long section, from 36 minutes in to approximately one hour 35 minutes, split into many sequences and filled with numerous 'little stories', shows the laborious approach to a hill numbered 210, its ascent and eventual capture. The Japanese have established a bunker on

Tall and Staros confront each other

this hill, from which they protect access to their airport. The attack is ultimately victorious, but also proves costly in human lives. In particular, it provides the occasion for a confrontation between Staros, concerned for the lives of his men, and his direct superior in the hierarchy, Tall, who wants them to make a frontal attack that Staros regards as suicidal. Meanwhile, Witt is reinstated in the company. In this section, he almost becomes just another soldier. We are more interested in Staros, in Private Bell (reduced to the ranks because of his love for his wife) and minor characters such as Keck, who dies to protect his companions from a mistake he has made.

However, in the middle of this section there is a second 'dialogue' between Welsh and Witt.

4. The fourth section, shorter and fragmented, is located near the capture of hill 210. The American soldiers take possession of a Japanese bivouac, which completes their momentary victory. C Company is awarded a period of rest. Staros is relieved of his functions. Welsh and Witt talk for a third and last time.

5. As they travel down a river towards the coast, where the boat will pick them up, C Company – or what's left of it – is attacked by the Japanese. Witt sacrifices himself to distract their attention and save his companions. At his graveside, Welsh spends a moment thinking of him one last time. We witness the transfer of power after Staros's departure and the embarkation of the soldiers for whom the war is over, each with his own experience. We also hear Witt's voice describing an experience of paradise in the form of a prayer. Then his voice stops and for the second time we see images of the Melanesian paradise.

Taken in isolation, the beginning and end of the film would suggest that *The Thin Red Line* is the story of Witt; however, it is certainly not the story of a man finding redemption and, by his death, saving not just two soldiers but also Welsh's 'soul', as one French critic has described it:

Like Christ, Witt will die to redeem the crimes and sins of men. A new departure then becomes possible; Witt's disciples (his companion in mutiny, the young WASP soldier, Staros, and above all Welsh/Sean Penn) will spread his message of love and peace.[3]

I do not agree with this idea of a 'message of love'. In my view, Witt is no kind of model, preacher or 'saviour'. If the film shows us anything, it is that each person's salvation, if there is one, is defined for and by that person and takes the most diverse paths, including the performance of acts of cruelty (for Dale), and solitude. No one can know how salvation is brought about for anyone other than themselves, or have any power to decide it, or claim to control it. To borrow the words of the French version of 'The Internationale', (without seeking to turn *The Thin Red Line* into a communist film), 'There is no supreme saviour,/ Not God, nor Ceasar, nor tribune.'

Alone

Alone. Each and every one of us is alone before the world, and death.

It is perhaps not immediately apparent, seeing *Badlands* again, that human solitude would turn out to be one of Terrence Malick's main motifs. Yet, watching carefully, in the light of the films that came after it, one may be struck by the particular sensitivity with which Malick films some of the minor characters – such as Kit's friend Kato, whom Kit kills and who lives alone, or the rich man in his house – and by the impression of distress and abandonment they convey.

In *Days of Heaven*, the main couple, played by Richard Gere and Brooke Adams, are curiously bland, despite the beauty and skill of the two actors. By contrast, the three characters who gravitate around them are far more emotionally involving, with an extraordinary presence; this is because each of them, in their own way, has a sense of loneliness: the old man who looks after the farm and suffers from seeing the death of its owner, whom he loves like a son; the young farmer played by Sam Shepard, unloved and fatally ill (the shots of him before his marriage to Abby or, after they are married, when he looks from a distance at the wife who is cheating on him); and of course little Linda, whose photo, mixed in with 'period photos' in the title sequence, shows her alone and already

abandoned. Paradoxically, Linda is rarely alone; usually she is seen in relation to others, on whom she seems dependent – but inside, in her rasping voice, she is alone from the beginning.

The Thin Red Line also speaks of loneliness, although this is not necessarily obvious. Loneliness in the cinema is often associated with an urban setting and with the modern world. What is loneliness doing here, in this luxuriant nature, this situation of promiscuity and war, this largely fraternal cohabitation and solidarity between soldiers, who are far from insensitive and take care of each other, supporting the wounded or dying?

Linda Manz, already alone and abandoned at the end of the title sequence of *Days of Heaven* (O.P. Productions / Paramount Pictures Corporation, 1978). 'Lonely? Only around people ...'

But – and Sergeant Welsh is right to say it – we feel all the more lonely when we are with other people ('Only around people'[4]). In this collective, choral, symphonic film, in which men share a war, ordeals and food, each is thrown back on himself all the more harshly at one point or another. We are alone like Witt when we visit the Melanesians who were once so friendly and are now afraid of us; alone when, during an attack on an invisible enemy, we are wounded and about to die, while the others will go on seeing the sun. Lieutenant Colonel Tall is alone when he plays the part of the soldier reprimanding his troops, scolding them for their slovenly dress or slackness, while in counterpoint we hear his inner voice saying, 'Shut up in a tomb … Played a role I never conceived,' which

A young Melanesian boy is afraid of Witt. The light of a candle – reflection of a divine flame?

prevents us identifying him with what he is doing, by showing us the
mismatch between his inside and outside. McCron (John Savage) is alone
and walled up in his madness, surrounded by his comrades, speaking his
monologue out loud (and not inside 'his head'): 'We're just dirt!' Alone, of
course, before an enemy who talks to us and doesn't understand us, whom
we do not understand, to whom we cannot even communicate the hatred
or resentment he inspires in us.

The Thin Red Line's long-awaited meeting with the Japanese enemy
is deferred for almost ninety minutes and, when it finally takes place,
breaks the illusion that he might have something to say to us and that we
can have something to say to him. These Japanese are all rigorously alone,
in their faith, their terror, their rage at being defeated; they don't face us,
we don't know who their leader is; they are examples of humanity, each
one a mirror for the solitude of the American soldiers.

The Thin Red Line shows us all these situations; for this film, in
which characters often do not have names and seem to be members of a
community, is also a film in which a large number of shots isolate each man
by turns, sometimes with the voice that speaks within him, in his suffering,
his fear, his incomprehension and also in the images that are dear to him,
that sustain him and him alone: a little photo he keeps in his pocket; a
letter read a hundred times; the light of a candle – just one, no more – in
which a Christian seeks the reflection of the divine flame from a darkness
in which the god he prays to does not answer; a memory which is his alone

Defeated Japanese soldiers: rigorously alone in their faith and their terror

and which he can't describe or at any rate pass on to anyone else – Bell's memory of his wife in the bedroom, or walking into the sea and turning back towards him with the skirt of her dress wet …

This is a war film in which we almost never see a troop of men together. There are no collective ceremonies, or rather they are reduced to a minimum, shown briefly in a kind of dream. Most often, in scenes of general joy and shouting (the distribution of letters, the joy of soldiers at last granted leave and even some group massacres, such as the attack on the Japanese bivouac), the sound of the group is muffled, dampened, heard from afar; we can't get involved in it, we are distanced. The single exception is the song in 'another language', the Melanesian song – the only time human voices, male and female, come together, the only chorus in the film. But it is sung in a language that is closed to us.

Perhaps if we did understand this song we would be disappointed, feeling we had been thrown into a new linguistic prison, since every language is both a world and a prison. From time to time we all need to be immersed in a language we don't understand, in which we see the paradise lost (which is why it would be a curse to understand the language of birds, like Siegfried in Wagner's opera, while the dream of such understanding is a blessing).

The men do not think together, or pray together. Often, when one speaks or tells a story, the other says nothing. The illusion of communication through dialogue does not last long. It is even shorter-

Bell's memory of his wife

lived when we meet our fellow, our brother, and he speaks, and we do not understand.

In a particularly important, powerful scene, two men, one of whom is temporarily the victor and survivor, the other the vanquished, are unaware that they are each saying the same thing in two different languages. Understanding is impossible on either side, and their loneliness would be all the greater if they understood and knew they were echoing each other.

And the music! Often in films, music brings people together and unites them, makes them dance or move together, breathe together. Here the music is at once compassionate and anonymous; it follows a rhythm that is not that of the action. It is a great, disconnected question.

Illusory Fusion

The lost paradise for which Malick's films, and particularly *The Thin Red Line*, make us long is among other things that of fusion with the other, with the person who is close to us or loved. The film makes us dream of this fusion while at the same time showing us how illusory and precarious it is.

The first occurrence of Linda Manz's narrative voiceover in *Days of Heaven* consists of words spoken by a child's voice, stating precisely, in a strong Chicago accent, 'Me and my brother, we used to be me-and-my-brother.' These words are heard over images showing the big brother with whom Linda says she lived in a fusional togetherness. But, instead of seeing Bill-and-Linda, we see Bill attacking a foreman in the factory where he works, which means he has to run away. On the one side is the voice, in the sound; on the other is the present action, in the image and also a little in the sound. There is no communication between them. But we can still believe that Bill and Linda are alone in the world and entirely complicit with each other.

Immediately afterwards we see Bill in a train talking to a young woman of his own age, Abby, whom he passes off as his sister, but who is really his girlfriend. For the little girl, 'me-and-my-brother' is no longer possible. Yet her rough voice goes on, speaking of Bill: 'He used to amuse us, he used to entertain us' – the 'us' here of course referring to the two female characters in the trio, Abby and Linda herself. Implicitly, it seems Linda's voice has conceded that her 'me-and-my-brother' is a fairy tale and is reassuring herself with the idea of a different, fusional 'us' formed by herself and Abby. At the same time, the film's image track occasionally, and fleetingly – for a few seconds – shows both the 'me-and-my-brother' the voice spoke of and the implicit 'me-and-Abby'. At the end of the film, Linda, who has lost her brother and been left in an institution by Abby, grafts herself onto another friend older than herself, of whom she says naively, 'She was a good friend.'

'Who's killing us?' asks an inner voice in *The Thin Red Line* just as the Americans are overrunning an undefended Japanese bivouac, in which

'Who's killing us?' Bell, alone with his wife's letter

many of the enemy are killed and others taken prisoner. Who is the 'us' at
this moment?

In reality *Badlands*, *Days of Heaven* and *The Thin Red Line* are all
concerned with illusory fusion – the painful realisation that one has gone
through the most gruelling ordeals with another person, 'together', and
that now it's over, the destinies are cruelly separating. In *Badlands,* the
destinies of Holly (Sissy Spacek) and Kit separate absolutely (he is found
guilty, she is acquitted); but throughout the film, Holly's voice has already
separated the couple by relating her point of view, which cannot be shared
with anyone, including her lover and the viewer, hindering any feeling we
might have that they are somehow twins.

In the first two films, the audience's illusory fusion with the
characters is also disturbed: we are distanced by the story they tell, which
is too personal, too closed, sometimes even autistic. In the third film,
matters become more complex and apparently the opposite occurs:
through the situations and speech, which convey universal questioning,
we can each identify with everyone in the film, although very few who
see it have risked or will risk encountering death and war of the kind it
shows.

Bell thinks of his wife: 'Why should I be afraid to die? I belong to
you.' Then he receives her letter in which she says she is leaving him. After
this he is 'reduced to the ranks'. Marty Bell's letter of separation kills the
illusion of the perfect, eternal, fusional love ('one being') and sends her

Powerless, Witt watches his comrades suffer and die

husband into absolute loneliness: at the same time, it creates between them an accord beyond life and death: 'Oh, my friend of these shining years!'

Suffering – here primarily the physical suffering of the wounded and dying, which the film says much about, along with fear – causes absolute separation. In the man who sees another suffering, it creates a feeling of almost total powerlessness to lessen that suffering, and in the one who is suffering, a symmetrical sense of powerlessness to speak of his suffering or to share it.

The paradox of the human condition is that we all suffer without distinction – the film continually reminds us of this – and the thing that makes us all fellows in our fate is also the thing that drives us apart as we experience it.

Malick's shooting and editing constantly emphasise that every person is alone in their skin, their hopes, their fear and their position. Strangely, however, this is not the feeling we are left with on leaving the cinema, or when the tape or DVD of the film comes to an end. But let us look carefully: at some time or another, almost all the characters are left alone with their actions, their thoughts, their uneasiness, and also with their decisions. 'Tough part is not knowing if you're doing any good,' says Staros to the soldiers who thank him for saving their lives by refusing to carry out Tall's order. Surrounded by his men's gratitude, Staros reminds us that at that moment he was more than ever alone.

The same sight is seen differently by different men, thinks Welsh: 'One man looks at a dying bird and thinks there's nothing but unanswered pain. But death's got the final word. It's laughing at him. Another man sees that same bird. Feels the glory.'

What binds men together is apparently their common loneliness, the certainty that one day they will have to die.

In the final embarkation scene, in which the surviving soldiers sail away in a landing craft, their particular war over, we might think the ordeal has brought these men together, that it has made them into a family. Malick does all he can to shatter this illusion. First, he introduces a scene in which Gaff (John Cusack), in a soliloquy spoken into another soldier's

face, speaks of his youth (and once again we become aware that a man whose adult life has started in this horror cannot see the experience in the same way as a man of forty or fifty, such as Welsh, Staros or Tall), using him to articulate the particularity of each man's experience. Then he has Witt's inner voice ask a series of questions: 'Where was it that we were together? Who was it that I lived with? Walked with? The brother? The friend?'

Last, those who are the most together are those who most disagree but can talk about it: Welsh and Witt. Their conversations are not verbal duels, or barely so. On the one hand, generally, it is Welsh who speaks. On the other, these 'verbal duels' between Witt and Welsh are acted and staged with more nuances and reserve than were written on the page. When Witt arrogantly says, 'I'm twice the man you are', in the brig, or Welsh calls him a 'troublemaker' in the plantation, the scenes are filmed and acted with extraordinary restraint.

Unlike a great many war films, *The Thin Red Line* contains very few direct clashes between individuals. The only really serious dispute (Staros's decision to disobey Tall's orders) takes place on the telephone. The other episodes between two men where one clearly disagrees with the other are always also scenes of avoidance. The subordinate keeps his thoughts to himself, or expresses them reservedly.

And Malick's *mise en scène*, shooting and editing emphasise both the isolation and vulnerability of each.

'Where was it that we were together?'

The sunlight catches soldiers from behind

Seen from Everywhere

The Thin Red Line is a war film, an action film, in which we see the vastness of nature, explosions bursting from all sides, houses burning and extras appearing and disappearing. As a grand spectacle it has two peculiarities.

First, there are as many, if not more, close-ups isolating a character's face than shots bringing characters together or pitching them against each other (despite the CinemaScope format). Second, there is not a single shot taken from the air, for example from one of the planes we see flying overhead or taking off from the airport, like the one in which Staros leaves. With very few exceptions, everything is seen from grass-height, or slightly above. The special, highly mobile Akeela crane was never used to look down on the characters from a great height, turning them into ants;[5] we are almost always on their level.

On the other hand, from the beginning there are many shots of shafts of sunlight, seen from a low angle: as they filter through the thick foliage of enormous trees; or at dawn, as the sun appears above a peak, having turned the clouds red; or as a dying man sees it through the holes in the leaves of a tree; or as it filters through low-lying mist, which suddenly lifts, enabling the Japanese to attack the Americans; or as it passes through the water in which the Melanesian children are swimming with Witt.

In the sky, with the sun and in its direction, there are birds flying and

Shafts of sunlight viewed from a low angle

waiting – as Dale says to the Japanese prisoner – for men to be wounded and die so they can eat you raw.

In *The Thin Red Line*, the sunlight permeates everything. It pours into the hollow of the brig where Witt is detained; it is also present in the light of the match that Witt burns in his cell, and in the candle before which Staros prays alone; it is the light of fire. Light in Malick's work often comes as a shock, an intrusion, a pursuit, breaking and entering, sometimes rape:

• A group of men on reconnaissance, led by Bell, climb a slope. The sky is overcast but the clouds are moving and the sunlight catches them from behind.

• No one who has seen *Days of Heaven* could forget the shot of the valuable glass lost by Richard Gere, resting underwater on the river bed at night. What makes this such a magical image is that we have the impression that a ray of light from the full moon (which we saw in a previous shot) is striking the glass even at the bottom of the river. Nothing can be hidden.

• The rich farmer's house in *Days of Heaven*, based on a famous painting by Edward Hopper, is filmed mainly from the outside. There are many evening or night shots showing the house lit up, with people moving inside, visible through the windows and curtains. These images repeatedly suggest that the house cannot deflect prying eyes.

The camera angles and movements in *The Thin Red Line* emphasise that the characters can be seen from any point in space. The world of the film is 360 degrees open.

This is signalled on several occasions by the characters. In the boat at the beginning, Quintard says to the lieutenant colonel, 'There's always someone watching.' Later Nick Nolte, who is himself using binoculars to watch a distant battle in which he is not physically engaged, reminds Staros that he must capture the target, as the admiral is watching: 'Now, goddamn it, the Admiral got up at dawn for this!'

In the middle of the firing, a soldier observes, 'One spot's as good as

another, men. There's no place to hide.' And the editing follows these
words with a shot bathed in sunlight falling vertically from the sky onto a
young man who is wounded and dying.

In the attack on the Japanese bivouac, in which wounded soldiers are
caught by surprise, naked and unarmed, visibility is lethal. Those whom the
camera finds and approaches, who look straight into it, are struck down.

In the long sequence of the capture of hill 210, the soldiers are thus
surrounded by different watching eyes: those of Lieutenant Colonel Tall,
who is following events from below with his binoculars;[6] those of the
Japanese, who are shooting at them from above; that of the sunlight falling
vertically; and lastly that of the camera, which catches them from all kinds
of angles – not to mention the eyes of the American admiral, mentioned
by Tall, who is watching it all from the sea.

Thus there are no shots, or very few, that are not at the level of the
mud, the water, the ground, the human being in the grass.

All human beings have walked in grass as high as themselves – at
least I should hope so. This Pacific island to which the American soldiers
have come to make war plunges them into a natural environment where
they often find they are smaller than the plants, the grass, like the children
they once were, like Witt as a boy looking at a big haystack during harvest,
in a remembered image that we see of him as a child.

Days of Heaven: a glass on the riverbed at night

When we grow up, something happens that adults don't talk about or don't remember: the world gets smaller. From then on everything is in some sense distorted, and this may help to make the world slightly disappointing.

Cinema returns objects to a larger size and, at the same time, may mix up scales.

Before cinema, phenomena of different scales could be made comparable only by words, particularly the words of poetry. Cinema has the privilege of being able to do this too; but it takes on a special meaning in a place like the Solomon Islands.

Visibility is lethal. American soldiers smaller than grass

In some countries, the vegetation is very tall and even an adult is no taller than a blade of grass; in others, the vegetation is smaller and, as they grow, adults lose their former similarity of scale with plants and flowers. In countries such as Iceland, the latitude and climatic conditions mean that a tree is often not as tall as a fully-grown man. How could nature not be perceived differently there; how could life not be essentially different?

The Haunting Beauty of the World

The beauty of the world is haunting in Malick's films – but do the characters notice it? One French critic observes:

Whereas in *Badlands* in particular, and to a lesser extent in *Days of Heaven*, the attention paid to nature – through inserted shots of flora and fauna – was that of the director alone (it was Malick looking at all that surrounded his characters), in *Thin Red Line* Witt becomes the prime observer of nature and it is most often through his eyes that we see a bird fly off, or the wind whispering in the trees and reeds.[7]

This is interesting, but possibly untrue – unless we identify Witt's viewpoint with the general view of the camera, which nothing suggests we should. There are many shots in which animals look. At what? The editing does not enable us to decide whether the animal really is looking and

The animal's impenetrable gaze

exactly what it sees. The animal's impenetrable gaze questions that of human beings.

The world we admire does not need to be looked at to be beautiful. The world does not cease to live because men are making war: the wind continues to blow, the grass to wave, the sun to appear and disappear behind the clouds and to brighten the colours of the world; the dawn continues to break.

But of course, nature is not idyllic. The film's first images – a crocodile slowly sinking into dark water, quintessential symbol of the predatory animal with which no pretence of communication is possible; trees covered in parasites – and the words spoken over these images (an 'inner voice' saying, 'What's this war in the heart of nature?') tell us this at once. The animals are at war; so are the men, and the plants. War is not a thing invented by human beings.

Malick does not contrast a good, peaceful nature with human beings who sully and profane it with their murders. What are a few burned trees compared to naturally occurring forest fires? Nature is beautiful, but it is not thought to be good. It has inspired the most beautiful of human words ('*Eos rhododaktylos*', the rosy-fingered dawn that Homer speaks of, quoted by Tall), but the words are human.

As in Malick's other films, the many 'inserts' of animals, which do not hide the fact that they have been included by the editing (animals are rarely present in the image at the same time as human beings), are there to

The film's first image

recall the existence on earth of other species that fly, swim or creep – in short, that live.

Another contemporary film-maker, Shohei Imamura, does this systematically, particularly in his version of *The Ballad of Narayama* (1983). In Imamura's work, the editing makes frequent parallels between human life and that of animals. Human creatures couple, animal creatures couple; humans eat other species and so do other animals. In Malick's work, by contrast, there is no parallelism, let alone any metaphorical use of animals (such as: man is a crocodile).

In Malick's work, animals do not speak at all – or very little. Is this an odd thing to say? Not really. Where, in many films, there is an emphasis on the barking of dogs, the chirping of birds or the stridulation of insects, Malick reminds us that for us humans, the talking-creatures, Lacan's *parlêtres* ('talkbeings'), animals are sometimes known as 'dumb beasts'. Canaries chirrup in a cage at the time of the memory of the mother's death, but as we hear them they are 'muted', discreet, they do not mingle their voices with the human voice, do not pretend to answer it. There are parrots in *The Thin Red Line*, but they do not imitate the human voice; there are birds that fly without calling, there are bats, a lizard, the voiceless crocodile and, at the end, as the penultimate image, a magnificent pair of parrots with the colours of paradise, but no call. This is quite unlike many anthropomorphist films which, in showing animals wild or domestic, make the cats miaow, the dogs yap, the hedgehogs groan and the birds sing, where the absence of the gift of language in animals is forgotten in order to persuade us that the animal hears what human beings say and speaks to them.

Just as in *Badlands* Holly's dog was dumb, so the crocodile is a dumb beast.

Human, plant or animal, we all live in the same world. But that's all we can say. It is in the image of this world of superimposition and juxtaposition, this world of parataxis, where ties of cause and effect and relationships between cohabitants are problematic, that Malick's cinema is built. In it, the 'door' opened to an understanding of our animality and our humanity by the Darwinian theory of evolution seems to have closed.[8]

How Big is a Crocodile?

In *Badlands*, Malick follows the image of Holly's mouth blowing cigarette smoke over Kit's ears with that of the mouth of a catfish, much smaller than Holly, but in an aquarium that is far too small for it: animality is never far away.

How big is a crocodile? This is the kind of question that, with cinema, we forget to ask ourselves. How long is the crocodile that sinks slowly into dark water at the start of *The Thin Red Line*, when compared to a human being? The image can't tell us. Encyclopaedias will inform us that, depending on species and region, these animals are between two and five metres long. In the film, we do not see the relative size of the animal until later, when one of its species is captured, surrounded by mute human beings.

The catfish in an aquarium too small for it: *Badlands* (Pressman-Williams Enterprises, 1973).
The size of a crocodile surrounded by mute human beings

Does the size of animals matter? It does in Malick's work, where the editing continually juxtaposes animals at different scales. But this juxtaposition of scales stresses the absence of communication – unlike folk and fairy tales in which species large and small, earthly and heavenly, animal and human, communicate and talk to each other.

From a distance, the Melanesian man who passes the first American soldier on the track leading inland seems to be so small only because he is far away. We think that, as he gets closer, he will attain the size of the soldiers he passes by. But when he draws level with the American, we see that he is small for a human being. We also see that he doesn't look at the westerners, that he doesn't speak to them, that he seems not to see them.

Badlands begins with a very strange scene, almost mythological beneath its appearance of charming cosiness, highlighting the respective scales of a human being and a domestic animal. In a girl's pretty bedroom, on an iron bedstead, Sissy Spacek, in the role of a girl of fifteen, plays with a spotted dog as big as herself. She talks to it in a childish way – we hear the story told by her narrative voice rather than what she says – and shakes her canine companion's paw as the camera turns, making us feel the private, enclosed aspect of the scene. The shot fades to black just as Holly is clearly lying with her dog – in the same way that films sometimes fade to black at the most private, crucial moment of a couple's embrace.

Holly and her dog in *Badlands*

But in this first image in Malick's cinema, woman and animal appear in the same shot, disturbingly complicit. There are no other examples of such a 'primal scene' in his work.

Malick is not implying some vulgar zoophilia here. It remains a game. Children often play with toy or real animals as big as themselves. In *Days of Heaven*, Linda asks her friend the farmhand, 'What happened to your ear?' The girl replies, 'A dog bit me when I was little. We were playing.' In Malick's work, play is the starting point for the vocation of the adult.

Playing, Working, Fighting

What Malick's first two films very clearly have in common, as we have seen, is the presence of a female narrative voice belonging to a character who is too young or immature to be responsible for the tragedies and horrors in which the male protagonist is implicated, and who tends to see life as a big game. Holly, in *Badlands*, thinks she is living a great fairy tale. 'He used to juggle with apples, he used to amuse us,' says little Linda Manz of her big brother in *Days of Heaven*, as he and his girlfriend go off to get work as farm workers.

Similarly, there is no transition between 'working' and 'playing'. Through editing and many temporal ellipses, the first part of *Days of Heaven*, which depicts the harvest, continually moves backwards and

Working and playing in the same place: the farm workers in *Days of Heaven*

forwards between times of work (and we see, we know that the farmhands work hard from dawn to dusk) and briefer moments of relaxation in the same places: dancing, doing cartwheels, playing baseball, swimming, until you might think these people had come to the countryside to have fun.

In Malick's work, play has a primal quality. It is not a preparation for life, a simulacrum of what people will do later 'for real', it is not pedagogical – it is the expression of life itself. The ideal, for Linda, and also apparently for Witt, is 'just nothing to do all day but crack jokes and lay around'.

At the start of *The Thin Red Line*, beautiful, living human children are crushing some kind of fruit under stones. We might think they are playing, but perhaps they are working to prepare food. A few seconds later, they rhythmically place these stones on top of other stones and play a kind of circular game. Is this a game or a ritual? The passage from one to the other is imperceptible. In the Melanesian tribe, it is hard to know what is work and what is play.

Play can be aggressive: how can we tell the difference between play fighting and real fighting? Animals can't. In *Badlands*, Kit and Holly play at throwing stones at each other; Holly's father plays at throwing paint on her bare legs, and there's sexuality too, a current of oedipal love between father and daughter.

It is when he moves into the war film genre with *The Thin Red Line* that Malick shows play tipping over into something else.

Is the Melanesian child working or playing?

We are used to seeing children's games – particularly territorial and war games – as manifesting both the sublimation and imitation of adult wars. But this is to forget that all adults began by playing, including those who make war as adults, whether by choice or not. Man makes war to go on playing, and it's no longer a game.

And yet it is. Lieutenant Colonel Tall is as excited as a child at the idea of 'taking hill 210', and not just because he may get promoted and so avenge his many years spent going nowhere in the army. We sense the strange certainty that human beings are not made to work or learn, but to play in the garden of the world: to play like Witt, with water, using his canteen to water a great leaf that seems to have no need of it.

Play without aggression, life without combat: are such things possible?

'Kids around here never fight,' says Witt at the start of the film to a beautiful, luminous Melanesian woman holding a baby girl in her arms. The woman replies (we don't see her speak, but the edit shows Witt hearing): 'Sometimes. Sometimes when you see them playing.' There is a pause, then: 'They always fight!' A strange, beautiful disjunctive edit ['*faux-raccord*'] follows: the woman laughs.

In Malick's work, war is close to play: there seems to be no profound difference between children who take the world or a corner of the earth for their playground, and put borders round it, and someone who decides that a hilltop is a strategic point.

'When you see them playing ... They always fight!'

In a scene from *The Thin Red Line* following the bloody, destructive fighting, as Witt walks around in the open, a soldier, who was already there alone, says, as though in play, 'I'd have had you Witt, if you was a Jap' – if it had been a war. At once the world has become a playground again, an open, non-delineated space.

The adult who makes war imitates the child he once was and not the other way round. It's just that here the consequences are different and terrible.

Paradise in Three Dimensions

Guadalcanal is an island. This is signified in words several times in the film, but it is never visualised. The viewer barely has time to glance at the map shown by John Travolta to prove the strategic importance of his conquest. At the same time, the theme of the island runs throughout the film in different forms: Welsh, in his second and last monologue, says that salvation is to 'make an island for himself'. As we have seen, the camera indicates that the space is surrounded. In the conversation between Nick Nolte and John Travolta, we might feel (through the way that Malick has filmed the conversation and the ship's bridge, and through the sounds that enter the space) that danger or a look might come from anywhere, even though the general does not utter the crucial phrase alluding to an admiral who sees everything and whom we never see.

The only image of the island

I have already noted that the film never gives us the falcon's or tree's point of view. Even though in some ways the audience is like the admiral or the falcon, sheltered from the dangers facing the characters they watch, they cannot slip into the distant, disengaged position of an observer of the world watching from afar.

The film's last image shows a tiny island – a plant on a fragment of rock. The film begins with water, continues on land, sets its final episode in the waters of a river and ends in water. It has made its characters cross first a plain, then a river, then it has made them climb higher and higher to reach the bunker. But when they get there, Malick avoids any images that might give an impression of dominance in relation to the surrounding space, in which the soldiers might feel that they are masters of that space. In his work, human beings never conquer space; they only meet other human beings.

In *The Thin Red Line*, only rarely do we see a space marked out by a human being.

The image often associated with American cinema is that of the road or trail: a route crossing virgin landscape, with telegraph poles, wires, a metallic voice sent over thousands of kilometres; that is American cinema itself.

Even in *Badlands*, which could pass for a road movie, Malick's cinema shows a minimum of roads and trails. Whenever they can, its characters move off on to unmarked ground, into virgin territory, fields and deserts; even in a river bed they move in circles, not straight lines.

A striking scene from *Days of Heaven*, shot with a Panaglide,[9] shows Richard Gere and Brooke Adams walking on the bed of a shallow river, with the camera turning around them. This scene is memorable for the way that the characters and camera use the space of the river freely and without moving in any specific direction.

Malick's use of camera movements, developed from his second film onwards, is not merely spectacular; it recalls that the space is not delineated, that we are free to cut through it, to come and go here and there, like Kit's car driving away from marked roads.

In Malick's work, the space of the land is shown as equivalent to the surface of the sea, where one can move through 360 degrees. Only swimming underwater, shown with grace and beauty at the beginning and end of *The Thin Red Line*, offers human beings the paradisiacal freedom of moving through three dimensions.

There are images of trails and paths in *The Thin Red Line*, but they are far more rare than is usual in war films. Whenever he can, Malick leads his characters into unmarked spaces, such as water, sometimes the sea.

The place of roads in Malick's films is taken by rivers, which do have a direction. Rivers play an important role in each of his three films: Martin Sheen camps on a river bank; Richard Gere and Brooke Adams have important conversations with their feet in the river; the scene of Witt's sacrifice takes place in a river and then not far from its bank.

However, it is a road that marks the end of *Days of Heaven*, or rather a railroad. As at the end of a film by Chaplin (as I mentioned earlier, the film quotes *The Immigrant*), a train carries away two vagabonds – Linda and her new friend – before the final credits.

Monologues are Islands of Words

Is *The Thin Red Line* an *Iliad*? It has often been called one, but to me the comparison seems only partially valid. The film has an epic form, made of small, cruel, familiar details and lyricism. Yet, though Tall quotes Homer on the field telephone ('rosy-fingered dawn'), nature plays

Underwater swimming: the paradisiacal freedom of moving through three dimensions

only a small part in Homer's poem, where it is immediately mythologised and personified, while in the film it is present everywhere, opaque and mute.

The Thin Red Line is certainly a poem, both in its lyric form and because the interior monologues scattered through it are like short pieces of naive poetry, islands of words in space. The film's images and music often act as space, allowing the words to emerge and be restored to their purity, just as the words of poems emerged from the blank page with the advent of print.

As a result, as in poetry, the most simple words become untranslatable. As a Frenchman, writing this book in French so it can then be translated into English, but starting of course from the English script, I despair of being able to translate the film's final monologue into French:

> Oh, my soul,
> Let me be in you now,
> Look out through my eyes,
> Look out at the things you made.
> All things shining.

Here are, respectively, the version dubbed into French and the subtitled version on the same DVD. Version dubbed into French:

'All things shining'

Oh, mon âme,
Recueille-moi maintenant.
Regarde à travers mes yeux
Les choses que tu as créées.
Tout est lumineux.

Close translation back into English:

[Oh, my soul
Gather me up now.
Look through my eyes
At the things you have created.
All is luminous.]

DVD subtitles:

Oh, mon âme,
laisse-moi pénétrer en toi.
regarde à travers mes yeux.
Regarde les choses que tu as créées.
Toutes choses resplendissantes.

Close translation back into English:

[Oh, my soul,
let me enter into you.
Look through my eyes.
Look at the things you have created.
All things resplendent.]

Of course the word *créer* ['to create'] is far too grand in French, but *faire* ['to make'] would have been too trivial (it might be said that one peculiarity of the French language is the frequent lack of a 'neutral' style between the familiar and the noble). In the subtitles, the grand – and beautiful – adjective *resplendissant* ['resplendent'] compensates for the vague nature of the word *chose* ['thing'] in French. And of course, 'let me' is untranslatable into French – or any other language (the French *laisse-moi* is too passive, *fais-moi* ['make me'] would be too active). The English participle 'shining' is similarly impossible to translate.

The Voice and the 'moving box'

The inner voices of *The Thin Red Line* seem to have cinematic precedents. One example is David Lynch's *Dune* (1984),[10] in which the director uses inner voices to render his characters' streams of consciousness, given in italics by the novel's author, Frank Herbert. But fundamentally, in both the novel *Dune* and Lynch's strange, beautiful film adaptation, the inner voice is the equivalent of the theatrical and operatic aside found in Molière or Mozart: it is usually a reaction to the situation in which the characters find themselves, a deliberation before action. This is not true of *The Thin Red Line*, where the voices do not necessarily have any precise connection to the exact moment into which they are edited.

The voiceover or inner voice that is 'out of line', whose relationship to the course of the narrative is non-linear, is the most striking and noted feature of Malick's cinema from *Badlands* on, with major differences between the first two films and the third.

In the first two, there is a single voice, which is female. In the third, there are many, and, with one exception (the voice of Bell's wife), they are all male. While the voiceovers of Sissy Spacek in *Badlands* and Linda Manz in *Days of Heaven* are, or seem, egocentric, those of the soldiers in *The Thin Red Line* are not always so: Tall talks about himself; others about what they feel about war; some meditate on life; Welsh's voice is sometimes polemical ('They lie').

The female voices of *Badlands* and *Days of Heaven* tell their story in the past tense with a certain nostalgia; the interior monologues of *The Thin Red Line* use the present tense – a timeless present. They rarely recount anything, apart from Witt's voice, to some extent, at the beginning of the film, when he talks about his mother's death.

Curiously, this use of the interior monologue is reminiscent of silent cinema, both in its short, fragmented nature and often in the abstract, general content of the words we hear. But in silent cinema, there would be no need to give a precise identity to the author of the words. In silent films, the words or thoughts of the different characters are written in the same font; they retain a general character.

Not everyone in *The Thin Red Line* has the right to an inner voice, but these voices do not make those who have access to them into heroes set above the others. The gift of an inner voice, a gift that can be withdrawn, is as random as that of divine grace in certain Calvinist beliefs. Tall possesses one when he first appears at the beginning of the film, but it is 'taken away' from him later. Sergeant Welsh – who, independently of the realist, cynical opinions he professes, acts on several occasions with generosity, courage and self-sacrifice (relieving a soldier with stomach cramps from combat; running through the bullets, risking his life, to ease the suffering of a soldier screaming with pain) – does not have one, except on two occasions at the end of the film. But why does Doll have a voice and not Fife? Why does McCron lack the 'gift' of an inner voice, instead reduced to screaming his questions, his distress, his queries to the universe into the air: 'Who's deciding who's gonna live?' 'Show me how to see things the way you do.'

So the inner voices isolate the characters from each other: those who have them from each other, because they possess them at different times,

'Who's deciding who's gonna live?'

and those who have them from those who don't. They are contradictory because they ask general questions, but without sharing them with the other characters. They do not mingle with the surrounding air, as though they were enclosed in the 'moving box' that is the human soul. They come up against the wall, the uncrossable 'line' around the individual consciousness, even if Witt dreams of a collective 'big soul'.

Typical is the scene between Nick Nolte and John Travolta referred to earlier, in which, while Quintard does not have an inner voice, Tall does. Tall's 'thoughts' about his feeling of humiliation (that of an ageing soldier who has not risen very far through the ranks), combined with his reserved speech, reinforce the isolation of each of these characters from the other.

At one point, Tall's inner voice, articulated at a level even lower than his spoken voice, declares, 'Can't lift the lid.' The voice is enclosed. An inner voice does not turn the scene into one observed through that character's subjectivity, enabling us to see 'through their eyes'. There is no identification between the voice and the viewpoint of the camera.

So the voice of the interior monologue is not just an exchange between an individual consciousness, lost in the cosmos, and our own. It is also like a door that opens and closes on a dark interior. At several crucial moments in the characters' destiny, they are rendered speechless, possessing neither a spoken nor inner voice; we are doubly cast outside them, and at the same time in a better position to feel sympathy and compassion for them.

Having relieved Staros of his command, Tall sits alone

This is the case with Tall, when, after the painful order to relieve Staros of his command, we find him sitting on a chair, apparently exhausted, while Welsh reads his letter of congratulations to the men of Charlie Company. Or when Bell has just received the letter from his wife, whose contents we have learned from her voice: he becomes almost speechless with the others. And indeed, we have no further access to his inner voice.

Then of course, there is the moment when Witt is surrounded by Japanese soldiers who are threatening and aiming their guns at him. Here we have two forms of enclosure: on the one hand, he does not understand what they are saying to him (any more than members of the audience who do not speak Japanese), and on the other, his inner voice is not there. He is entirely closed to us, in the triple box of his non-comprehension of the language spoken to him by an enemy with a human face, his body that does not speak and his silent soul. What is he doing? What does he want? Does he aim his weapon deliberately, causing the Japanese to fire, instead of letting it fall? We shall never know.

Generally speaking, the film never gives us the thoughts of the dying, those whom we see dying, suffering, being dead, at the moment it happens to them: Keck, Tella, Witt.

The inner voice is not always 'iconogenic', to use a word I have proposed in *Un art sonore, le cinéma*.[11] In other words, it does not bring images with it, except fleetingly. When there is a flashback, the image seldom follows the voice.

Nor is the inner voice in the action; it provides a free, often atemporal commentary. It seldom reacts to what is happening or has just happened (except when Doll has just committed his first murder – 'I killed a man!' – or when Staros looks at his soldiers, whom Tall wants to send into the firing line: 'Children!').

What the voices say is simple, explicit, direct. They articulate the 'why's of early life, the questions of childhood that we keep alive and hidden within us throughout our lives, for our lives continually fail to answer them. But the clear, direct nature of these questions precisely indicates that nothing goes without saying and that, thanks to the voices,

because of the voices, all that we see and hear is a mystery. They highlight the false evidence of the visible.

Sometimes the editing gives a precise meaning to these errant words, fixing them to an individual face. When Doll's voice meditates on the fact that 'War don't ennoble men. It turns 'em to dogs. Poisons the soul,' the last three words are edited over the image of Dale, the most aggressive of the men, who mutilates a Japanese corpse in front of another, living Japanese soldier, and whom we later see weeping, in the rain, then silent.

The inner voice passes from one to the next, always moving on, so that these voices that are closed to each other at the same time combine into the modulated meditations of a single collective consciousness. They are like a single text that the voices share between them, like a shared reading – now whispered, now more peremptory, or more anxious.

In the logic of the film, it is out of extreme human isolation and insularity (each man is an island) that 'together-ness' can emerge.

A Continuum between 'speaking aloud' and the 'inner voice'

However, the distinction between the inner voice on the one hand and the film dialogue on the other is not always so clear. Through different means, Malick often creates the feeling of a continuum between the voice that speaks aloud and the meditative inner voice, while at other moments, the one is clearly distinct from the other and can even be superimposed on it,

'War don't ennoble men. It turns 'em to dogs.'

like a stranger. Witt 'thinks' over images in which he does not open his mouth. But we also see Staros talking out loud all alone, when he is praying.

Often one voice starts saying something in the present, without an image of the person speaking, and we might initially assume it is a thought, but immediately afterwards discover that it was said out loud in the context of a conversation. For example, Witt's account of the death of his mother seems to start in his head, or in a voiceover narration: 'I remember'. No, says the image, he is telling this story to his companion in desertion. Similarly, we might think Tall's quotation of Homer, heard over an image of clouds coloured by the rising sun, is the character's thought or school memory, until the editing reveals that he is talking to Staros on the telephone.

Scenes I remember as having dialogue are in fact monologues punctuated by 'Yes, sirs' and 'No, sirs' from the subordinate, like the three-part scene with General Quintard, in which he is practically the only one to speak, taking advantage of his rank and the presence of another man of inferior status to expound his ideas and feelings, with the disadvantage that he cannot have a dialogue with him – so much so that sometimes he both asks the questions and gives the answers: 'You wonder why ... Why did the Japs put an airfield there of all places?' When, after his fulsome and complacent monologue, the general asks Tall, 'What do you think?', Tall is careful to avoid giving a personal view and remains in

Staros prays

his place: 'Well, sir, I never ask myself the question.' But talking without a response makes Quintard appear as alone as the ageing and humiliated soldier before him. This scene between Travolta and Nolte is moreover a montage of various moments filmed in different lights. At the end, the two characters say almost nothing to each other, but we 'hear' Tall think.

Just after this, when we meet the soldiers of C Company, the scene again begins with a monologue – the torrential soliloquy of a frightened soldier who covers up his fear with a rush of words. This time Sergeant Welsh lets a private speak, inverting the more usual situation in the film.

Witt's account of the death of his mother, the second confrontation between Welsh and Witt, under the moon, the dialogue between Tall and

Alone together. Welsh lets the private speak

Gaff, in which Gaff says almost nothing, and Gaff's monologue in the landing craft that marks the first stage of his journey home, summing up his experience before the silent Dale, are all in fact monologues spoken out loud, which at least have the chance of being heard – unlike the inner voices, enclosed in a bubble of deafness.

Days of Heaven had many scenes of 'dialogue' in which one person merely listens, as when the old man who runs the farm is doing the accounts in the presence of Sam Shepard, or when Richard Gere is trying to persuade Brooke Adams to accept the advances of the rich young farmer. Many dialogues in Malick's films are in fact thus monologues, allowing the words to resonate in the silence of the 'interlocutor' – and echoing the intermittent interventions of the narrative voice or inner monologue.

Here again we return to the questions of loneliness, of the space between words and consciousness, and between languages.

Brother in Language

Enemies with two different languages face each other in two crucial scenes, in which Malick does not subtitle the Japanese dialogue (nor is it dubbed into the local language in dubbed copies), so that our point of view remains that of the Americans. Strangely, western commentators have shown no interest in what the Japanese are saying. I have asked a student to translate it.

When Dale sadistically tells the Japanese prisoner he is going to die, eaten alive by carrion birds, the prisoner repeats over and over that the American too will die one day. Neither expects to be understood by the other. It is this speech that will remain, these phonemes incomprehensible to Dale (*Kisamawa shinundayo*) that – as revealed in a brief flashback – he keeps within him without having understood them, embedded in him like blade, a dagger, a wound to the quick, which is for him a chance to live again as a human being, no longer dehumanised by the war. His tears, in which none of his companions join or sympathise with him, are the sign of his return to humanity.

In the scene in which Witt, who has distracted the attention of the Japanese soldier in order to save two men he has taken under his

protection, is surrounded by a group of Japanese soldiers in helmets camouflaged with branches, what one of the soldiers repeatedly says to him in Japanese is unequivocal: 'surrender' (*kufukushiro* – a brutal expression according to my translator Kazuko Nii). 'It's you who killed my friend in war. But I don't want to kill you [*ore wa omae o koroshitaku nai*], you are already surrounded. Surrender.'

What is striking here is that the soldier who is aiming at Witt does not take account of the likelihood that his enemy might have no understanding of these words spoken without hatred. He speaks to him 'directly' and openly – in other words incomprehensibly – and doesn't even try to make himself understood with gestures. He speaks as to a brother in language.

This is the mystery of language, which is the substance of our thinking. Language comes from the heart, and does not strike the heart. But how can we know this?

Sometimes a scene unfolds before our eyes but the voices and sounds are muffled, as though by a protective shell. The audience is protected from a cry that is too horrible, a sound that is too powerful, a folly that is too great. 'Making an island for oneself' to bear the horror.

The First Murder

In *Badlands*, Kit enters Holly's family home uninvited; her father (Warren Oates), opposed to his very young daughter's relationship with this young

Dale's grief

man with a bad reputation, catches him and asks him to leave. Kit warns him, 'I got a gun here, sir', before explaining that he is taking Holly away with him. The father takes no notice and again asks him to leave. Kit verbalises more clearly the fact that the father is ignoring: 'Suppose I shot you? How'd that be?' The father does not react. Kit fires the pistol at the ground ('Wanna hear how it sounds?'), still without hurting anyone, as though to make his words worthy of consideration. But the father remains unmoved, continuing to regard Kit as an irresponsible child. He turns his back and walks away. Kit shoots the father, who falls to the floor, dead.

The unreality in this scene arises from the fact that the murder and its instrument are announced in advance, as in a game, but it makes no

Witt and the Japanese soldier: brothers in language even though neither understands the other

difference, and this is why it is committed. Kit shoots as though that were the only way to make what he announced real. If his words had been taken seriously, there might have been no act. On the other hand, his behaviour immediately afterwards might seem offhand, lacking in all humanity, just as Holly's, in asking her murdered father, 'Are you gonna be OK?', seems infantile. Death is not named.

By contrast, *The Thin Red Line* seems to link the word murder to the word war – to remind us that war is not just killing, it is an accumulation of individual murders that are shocking every time, including for the killer.

'I killed a man. Worst thing to do. Worse than rape,' says Doll. The film has been running for fifty minutes; bullets have whistled, machine guns fired, grenades exploded, and these words are the last we are expecting to hear. Who are these war-film soldiers who are making such a fuss about killing a man? After all the films on all possible wars, after *Platoon* (1986) and *Full Metal Jacket*, what are all these feelings about?

It must first be said that we are not in Vietnam in the 1960s. This is 1942, with young American soldiers engaged in a war they have not seen on television.

But also we are dealing with a very particular director.

In most films, when someone is killed there's no need to say there has been a murder; in Malick's film, it is necessary and so, because of this very need to name the murder, to say, 'I killed a man', the act itself becomes ambiguous.

'I killed a man'

When children play at death, without committing it, they say death. This allows them to play with it. This poses the problem of video games, in which death is often dealt out to realistic-looking characters, without being named.

But immediately after the inner voice whose words we have reported, which intersects with words spoken aloud by Doll, we hear the latter say in himself, quickly, 'Nobody can touch me for that.' So it is not just that this is a murder, but that in wartime it's not possible to acknowledge it as such, to be disturbed by having committed it, and thus to be forgiven for it.

Doll's 'Nobody can touch me for that' is a strange echo of the words in Genesis when, by killing his brother Abel, Cain commits the first murder in the Bible: 'And the Lord set a mark upon Cain, lest any finding him should kill him.'

War takes murder out of any hierarchy and renders it unreal; there is no one to condemn murder in itself, and therefore no one to forgive.

In *Badlands*, Kit applies a strange morality to himself as events unfold: he feels no remorse for having killed three men, because they were not policemen but 'bounty hunters', yet he and Holly often surround the murders they leave behind them in silence or ambiguous words. One of the strangest moments occurs when Kit shoots twice, apparently at random, in the direction of the place in which he has asked a young couple to hide while he gets away. Immediately afterwards, Kit asks Holly, 'Think I got them?' and she replies, 'I don't know.' 'Well, I'm not going down there and look.' The rest of the film gives us no clue as to whether the young people were wounded, killed or unhurt.

The same unreality can be seen in *Days of Heaven*: after tying up his wife, the farmer aims his pistol at his rival, Bill, but we don't know whether he wants to use it. Then, after a brief and very confused struggle, Bill finds he has stabbed him, apparently without meaning to. He is now guilty of a murder that he will not name as such. All he says to Abby is, 'I'll tell you the whole story later', but nothing is ever revealed. Moreover, how is it possible to tell 'the whole story' of anything?

In the scene of the attack on the Japanese bivouac, Malick suggests the 'murders' of many unarmed and defenceless Japanese soldiers, cutting before the actual shot is fired. This could be put down to his visual restraint, but it also renders many of the murders unreal, which perhaps reflects how many soldiers feel about committing them.

Days of Heaven was an 'under-verbalised' film: we know that Richard Gere and Brooke Adams were lovers rather than brother and sister, but this was not really made clear, not really shown, not really said, except indirectly, via a perfidious remark from a farmhand or by the voice of Linda, a voice that contradicts itself, makes things up, fantasises, and is thus not trustworthy when it comes to facts. Bill and Abby, whom we never see making love, kissing or really embracing, even when they are alone and have no one's eyes to fear but ours, are as ambiguously positioned to us as to the other characters.

This 'under-verbalised' film in Malick's oeuvre is followed by one that is over-verbalised: everything is described in words after being shown. As a result, we continue to detect a lack of balance, an unease between words and actions. Does the word 'murder' make it murder? Isn't it clear enough that in war it's a question of kill or be killed?

Trace and Death, Immortality

Malick's three films also deal with the problem of memory, of traces (we should not forget that all three are set in the past).

In the first, again and again, we see that Kit wants to leave traces of his strange, bloody adventure, starting with a recording of his voice on a 'Voice-O-Graph' disc. This record, announcing his own and Holly's suicide, is intended to mislead the police, but he leaves it in the father's house before setting fire to it (without thinking that the recording will be burned too). Later, in the rich man's house, he speaks into a tape recorder microphone. Later still, while they are on the run, he buries objects to be found 'a thousand years from now'. Lastly, we should not forget the little heap of stones, a very temporary 'cairn' that he builds at the spot where the police eventually arrest him, before raising his hands in the air – as though he thought this simple 'monument' might last. Speaking about

Badlands, Malick told *Positif*, 'The feeling of sadness emanating from the film's conclusion stems partly from the fact that the girl, his best historian, is living a different life, so that his own story sinks without trace.' This is belied by the film itself, a trace of the traceless.

In *Days of Heaven*, the remaining traces of the period described appear only in the opening credit sequence; the rest of the film does not return to them. In a series of period photos, over which we hear a piece of music by Saint-Saëns, we see people from days gone by, all anonymous, who radiate a strange emotion. These are people who have lived and suffered, ordinary working people, people in the street, between whom there slips a fictional character, the muddled 'narrator' played by Linda Manz. She is a hallucinatory narrator whom we cannot trust to build a coherent, lasting story of the events she has largely witnessed. As is to be expected, when Bill is killed by his pursuer we are not present at any scene in which the survivors are interrogated; Bill's story seems to have been buried – no newspaper article constitutes his tomb, and later, neither Abby nor Linda refers to what has happened in words.

In many films by other directors, photos are often taken by the characters themselves or a professional photographer, representing a trace, however fragile, of what we have seen. In *The Thin Red Line*, the trace loses its materiality; there is no chronicler present, no photographer, no camera. When the soldiers leave, none of them remember the dead in words, yet it seems that, beyond any material or verbal monument, the life of those who are dead has passed on its spark to the living.

In his second monologue, after Witt's death, Welsh makes no mention of the name or memory of the man whom he has told himself was perhaps 'the best friend you ever had', but what he does say has changed.

The immortality of which Witt spoke at the start of the film, and which he did not see when his mother died, is this anonymous transmission of the spark of life.

Passing the Graves

Witt's makeshift grave, with his gun and helmet for a cross, is another trace, over which Welsh pauses for a moment in thought. So too are the

Welsh's face is lost in the image of C Company. Men come, one after another. Doll transfers his gaze to an arriving boat.

military graves, which the surviving soldiers pass without stopping on their way back to the ship.

The last interior monologue by a 'living person' in *The Thin Red Line* is given to Welsh. In themselves his words might indicate that his despair is greater than ever, but the speech is more complex and contradictory than that. Where other monologues in the film question or plead, this states; but its statements are those of a man whom we have seen in the film being courageous, benevolent towards others and always ready to talk or help – the opposite of a nihilist who keeps himself to himself, satisfied with the disorder and disaster in the world.

'Everything a lie. Everything you hear, everything you see. So much to spew out,' he says abruptly 'in his head', as with our other ear we follow George Clooney's words as he addresses his troops. We should be wrong, in my view, to apply this statement only to Bosche's speech, in which he asserts his authority, designating himself as the father and Sergeant Welsh as the mother (a phrase humorously laid over the close-up of a sceptical Sean Penn, sulking silently). For a moment, doubt is cast over all of reality and perception.

'They just keep coming, one after another.' The subject of the verb 'they' seems ambiguous, since it varies from one translation or foreign version to the next: 'It never stops, one lie after another' (French dubbed version) or 'Men come, one after another'. The latter perhaps more precisely reflects the film's rolling construction, its turnover of different characters, living and dead, those who have made war and those who are going to make it (later, from the stern of the boat leaving Guadalcanal, Doll transfers his gaze to a boat that is arriving). The end of the film is organised around an idea of people passing each other in opposite directions.

'You're in a box, a moving box.' This beautiful, mysterious phrase is again given a bizarre interpretation by one of the French versions, which translates 'box' as 'coffin', thereby restricting the meaning. In my view, the 'moving box' refers to human beings themselves, who feel confined within their own limits and aspire to escape them, letting what they feel to be 'their soul' fly off.

'They want you dead, or in their lie.' Shortly after 'in their lie' (another allusion to the idea of a box) begins a dissolve that 'melts' the character of Welsh into the troop of surviving soldiers from C Company as they march by a military cemetery. At this point, the monologue by Welsh, whom we shall not see again until he is in the landing craft, alone with his thoughts and silent amid the others, continues without his image, and we see, in one of the film's rare moments, a troop, organised and homogeneous.

'Only one thing a man can do: find something that's his. Make an island for himself.' At the end of these words, the moving camera centres for a moment on the character of Dale, silent and alone, who, like the other soldiers (but isolated from them by the framing for a few seconds), glances, as he marches by, at the new graves of those who have remained in this land. These words could be understood as the profession of a selfish faith, but the last sentence, over a shot of Dale seen from behind with his helmet (becoming the representative of all soldiers, and indeed all human beings), turns everything upside down. 'If I never meet you in this life, let me feel the lack.' In the image, the word 'lack' coincides with an interval during which one soldier leaves the frame to the left and no other has yet entered from the right,[12] so that we see only the graves.

The 'lack' is not only the graves that fill the vast CinemaScope screen for a second, it is an absence – that of our dead, recreated and revived when we think of them – that allows life to perpetuate itself. Here, through the editing of sound with image, the 'I' that is the subject of the sentence is no longer just the individual psychological character of Welsh. Just as when, later, the voice begins again, 'A glance from your eyes, and my life will be yours,' the word 'glance' accompanies an anonymous soldier gazing at both the graves and at a motionless Melanesian woman, in profile, who is not looking at the soldiers and is hidden for a while by a tree. She only turns towards the soldiers when the man who was observing her has already gone by. Two pairs of eyes almost met; it didn't happen, but perhaps another time it will.

Similarly, after 'yours', the shot ends with an image of the graves and the silent Melanesian.

In the second scene of the film, Welsh had told Witt that there is
only one world. This time, in saying 'this life', he leaves open the
possibility of another life, whether on earth or elsewhere.

Welsh is a good character, whom we would not wish to criticise, but
he has lost the feeling of lack. His prayer at the end is clear.

Signed: An Atheist of Nature
Some people are religious atheists, but are deeply moved by Bresson's
Diary of a Country Priest (1951) or Pasolini's *Gospel According to St
Matthew* (1964). I myself am an atheist of nature: I believe that nature is
not someone we can speak to or question, that nature is not singular

Two pairs of eyes almost meet

Three levels of life: human, animal, vegetable

and that the question of understanding whether it is singular or double has no meaning. And yet this film, particularly the end, part of which I have just described, touches me to the quick in the way that it shows the world, the beauty of plants, of the sky and sun, and, above all, of life.

It has perhaps as yet passed unnoticed that the last three shots of *The Thin Red Line* – in which Witt's voice is no longer heard, having fallen silent over the image of the boat's wake – show, in separate images united by a single emotion, three levels of life: human (children in a boat), animal (the pair of magnificently coloured birds) and vegetable (the plant above the water). This is a supposedly descending order, 'regressive' on the evolutionary ladder, yet it ends in beauty.

In James Jones's novel and the historical reality to which the book bears witness, we know that the nature of Guadalcanal was far more hostile and much less luxuriant, less staggeringly beautiful than it is for the audience of *The Thin Red Line.* But so what? The words Malick gives to Witt, in the last monologue, could also be applied to him: 'Look at all the things you made. All things shining.' His nature is beautiful because it is seen to be beautiful.

As a little girl in Vietnam, the writer Christiane Sacco, who was a very dear friend of mine, experienced the horrors of both war and nature at the same time (alone, her mother dead and her father a prisoner, she wandered through the hostile forest, eating roots and hiding from Japanese soldiers driven mad by war). She told me that for her, the only film to tell the truth about nature was John Boorman's *Deliverance* (1972), in which nature does not humanise human beings. She is no longer with us, but I think she would have liked *The Thin Red Line.*

For this film does not use images and sounds, history, the suffering of flesh and spirit, sensations and colours, cries and silences as a pretext to run away from words or to dilute their meaning in some great ambiguous mush. In Malick's work, as I have said, words never give up questioning and speaking; they go on to the end, or almost, like a beautiful boat with pure lines.

It is probably because of language that we feel we are part of the world without being part of it; language allows us to bless the world, to glorify its brilliance, but in the same movement it exiles us, because it is ours alone. This too is the earthly paradise lost: feeling foreign to the world that we admire, because we have language.

Cinema is the 'moving box' that can contain people and objects, things that exist and may have nothing in common ('What are you to me?'), starting with words and sensations. In the hands of Terrence Malick, this box becomes magic. The beauty of things, woven together with the beauty of voices and words, becomes once more alive and human.

Appendix: Synopsis

I have established this scene breakdown (which does not correspond exactly to the chapters of the DVD editions) in order to facilitate identification of the characters and scenes discussed in the course of this essay.

At the same time, the difficulty the viewer has, even after watching the film several times, in telling some characters apart, attributing some of the voices to their owners, knowing what is in the past and what in the present, following the course of events, gauging the duration of the action, understanding the topography of the island, and so on, is an integral part of the film. This synopsis is not intended to prevent anyone seeing the film in all the deliberate confusion of its narration.

I. BEFORE THE FIGHTING

1. Witt's paradise: 'Hidden immortality'

Images of nature in all its extravagance: a crocodile, trees, the sun (Witt's interior monologue on war in nature: 'Is there an avenging power in nature?').

Witt and another soldier are living in a peaceful Melanesian village, in harmony with its inhabitants.

He describes the death of his mother and his quest for the immortality that he did not see when she died (flashback images). An American patrol boat comes ashore.

2. Witt and Welsh in the brig: the man who sees only one world and the man who has seen another

Witt has been put in a cell as a deserter. His company sergeant, Welsh, observes that it's not the first time. He tells Witt that he risks court martial, but that he likes him and has managed to get him taken on as a stretcher-bearer in a disciplinary battalion. They exchange their conceptions of life: 'There ain't no world but this one,' says Welsh; 'I thought I seen another world,' says Witt; Witt to his cell-mate: 'I love Charlie Company, they're my people.'

3. Quintard and Tall: 'With the admiral watching'

On the bridge of a large warship off the islands, General Quintard and Lieutenant Colonel Tall discuss (mostly Quintard) the coming assault on the island of Guadalcanal, to be watched by the admiral: the aim is to dislodge the Japanese, who have built an airport on the island. We also learn that Tall, who is to lead the attack, is an ageing, bitter man, who has not received the promotion he had hoped for (Tall's interior monologue, suffering).

4. C Company: 'I just can't help now how damn scared I am'

Through short scenes on the boat, we meet the members of 'Charlie Company', along with their sergeant, Welsh, and Captain Staros. They are waiting to disembark, terrified and shut in under a low ceiling. In particular, we follow the story of Bell, whose love for his wife has led to his being reduced to the ranks (flashback images of her and a brief interior monologue by Bell). The soldiers are afraid of being attacked by planes, or of having to fight the Japanese on the beach. Each struggles in his own way with his fear of dying. C Company is afraid of always being in the wrong place at the wrong time.

5. Disembarking and heading inland: 'Your outfit is lucky'

The soldiers board open landing craft, where they pray, wait and look at the sky. Nothing happens. They land on an empty beach. The only person they meet on a track is a Melanesian native, who does not even look at them. Until now they have been lucky.

Afraid of being attacked by aircraft

They walk through trees, Witt's inner voice invoking nature: 'Who are you, to live in all that many forms?' Private Bell's memory-images: himself and his wife. The troop advances, passing through long grass, then through a muddy forest, and emerging high on a hill.

6. The wounded, 'all faces of the same man'

Further on, the soldiers come across bodies and wounded American soldiers. No dialogue tells us what happened. Witt the stretcher-bearer takes care of the survivors, comforting, washing and treating them on a river bank. The suffering of the wounded. Witt's interior monologue: 'Maybe all men got one big soul; all faces of the same man.'

II. ATTACK AND CAPTURE OF HILL 210

7. Hill 210: 'No way to outflank it'

Tall orders C Company to capture hill number 210 in a frontal assault, as there is 'no way to outflank it'. They must cross three small rises to attack the hilltop.

An image reveals in advance that a Japanese machine gun is waiting for the soldiers, poking through a slit in the wall. In vain, Staros explains that the men may not have enough to drink on their way up.

8. Staros's prayer: 'Are you here?'

We see Staros alone, at night, praying to God: 'let me not betray you'.

9. Dawn

Conversation at dawn on a 'sound power' (field telephone) between Tall (who quotes Homer) and Staros: we learn that the artillery is going to shoot from below to cover the American assault, but that, with little fire power, its main effect will be to 'buck the men up' and make them believe the Japanese are 'catching hell'.

10. First combat: 'I killed a man'

First explosions, first panics. Private Sico has stomach cramps. Sergeant Keck wants to force him to fight, but Welsh tells Keck to let him go to the medics. The first explosions, first bullets fired by the Japanese and incurred by the Americans. A man falls, then a second, then many. Panic. Staros roughly tells the stretcher-bearers to take care of some men rather than others.

Witt reappears with a rebellious attitude and asks Captain Staros to have him reassigned to the company as soon as his work as a stretcher-bearer is over. Staros agrees. Welsh seems put out.

Telephone call from Tall on the plain: he has 'seen everything' from down there, and does not understand why the soldiers have not yet located the source of the Japanese firing; he wants the hill taken that evening.

Private Doll identifies some Japanese and shoots. His first 'kill' ('I killed a man'). A group takes refuge in the shelter. Japanese soldiers arrive, they fire on them.

11. Death of Keck: 'You didn't let your brother down'

Violent exchange of fire. Keck makes a mistake, taking a grenade by its pin, and lies down so it will explode on him, sparing his comrades. He is seriously hurt; he is going to die. Witt looks after him and says: 'Even if you die, you didn't let your brother down.' Keck asks Doll to write to his wife, which Doll promises to do, but, once Keck is dead, he says he can't and doesn't want to do it.

Sergeant McCron, who has lost all twelve of his men, gradually goes mad.

12. Welsh's courage: 'Whole fucking thing is about property'

Private Tella has been wounded and is screaming with pain. He is going to die. How can they get morphine to him under the hail of bullets? Welsh makes a sudden decision: managing to get the morphine to him, he sees that he cannot be carried and says goodbye to him. Welsh returns. Staros congratulates him: 'I'm going to recommend you for the Silver Star.' Welsh is furious, refuses a medal and threatens to resign: 'Whole fucking thing is about property.'

13. Staros's refusal: 'I refuse to obey your order'. Death of a very young soldier.

Tall, from his position at the base of the hill, speaks to Staros on the telephone and demands that he make a frontal attack on the Japanese position. Staros tells him this would result in a massacre, that the Japanese have too much fire power. He suggests sending two groups on the flank, but Tall wants the whole unit to attack. Staros officially refuses. Tall: 'You must have a reason. I'm coming down, but I'm not rescinding my order.'

The fighting continues. A very young soldier is wounded and Staros, along with Private Fife, impotently watches him die.

14. Tall visits the line

Tall visits the line engulfed in smoke and reprimands the soldiers for their weakness (Tall's interior monologue: 'Playing a role I never conceived.') He finds Staros and is surprised that he has lost no men in the last ten minutes: 'the situation has changed, Colonel'. Tall gives the order to attack the ridge. McCron continues raving: 'We're just dirt.'

15. Bell on reconnaissance

Bell is sent off on reconnaissance with six men, including Witt, to find out where the Japanese are firing from; they crawl up through the grass. Then

Eos rhododaktylos: rosy-fingered dawn

Bell decides to go on alone (mental images of his wife back home in America, with her voice).

Eventually he finds the place by discharging a grenade and returns to the group: 'A bunker, five guns.'

16. Tall and Staros: 'How many lives?'

Tall addresses the men: the Japanese have left one side unprotected. The Americans must take advantage of this before they realise their mistake. He apologises for the lack of water; they have not been able to bring any up. Seven men volunteer for the attack.

Dialogue between Staros and Tall as they walk together – or rather, monologue by Tall: 'Guadalcanal may be the turning point in the war.' He asks Staros how many deaths he is willing to accept to achieve this end; Staros confines himself to saying: 'You are right, sir.'

17. The night before the attack: Welsh and Witt, McCron, Bell, Staros

Evening: calm, lovely light, open air. Welsh talks 'with' Witt, who says nothing. Welsh declares that you can't do anything for other people in this 'burning house' of a world. There is no other world. Witt looks at the moon.

Dogs are eating human remains. McCron shouts over the image of the scavengers: 'Who's deciding who's gonna live? I'm alive? Why?'

Welsh talks 'with' Witt, who says nothing

Monologue and memory-images of Bell with his wife in California: 'flow together; like water; till I can't tell you from me'.

Staros, alone, looking old, eats from his dish; he prays, alone, beneath the moon.

18. Capture of the bunker

C Company wakes up. A group including Witt, Doll and Bell is sent to find Captain Gaff. They approach the bunker, at dawn, without being seen. Gaff identifies the precise location of the bunker, which means it can be machine-gunned from below. Attack: Doll is very frightened, but overcomes his fear and attacks with a grenade. Intense, violent fighting ensues. The bunker is captured. The first Japanese faces appear. One soldier abuses the Japanese ('You pieces of shit'), or kills them. Bell is horrified. Staros stops him. Bell, to Doll: 'I shot a man.' The bunker is taken.

19. Prisoners

The Japanese prisoners, guarded by the Americans: one prays, another rages, another weeps. Witt gives cigarettes to a Japanese soldier (at least we think he does, because the reverse shot does not confirm it). The fighting begins again: rapid shot showing the clearing of Japanese hide-outs.

20. Tall and Gaff: 'Some day, you'll understand'

Tall arrives, noisily shows his satisfaction and offers Gaff a command. Gaff reminds him that the men need water. At first, Tall refuses, so as not to delay the final attack: 'I waited all my life for this.' Gaff says nothing. Eventually, Tall asks for water to be brought up and announces that the final attack will take place in one hour.

21. The dead: 'like dead dogs'?

Inner voice of Private Fife: 'You seen many dead people? ... They're meat, kid.'

Voice given to the face of a dead Japanese soldier sticking out of the ground: 'I too was righteous, I too was loved. Do you imagine your sufferings will be less because you love goodness? Truth?'

Fire. Distribution of bullets, the men arm themselves with bayonets.

22. The attack on the Japanese camp: 'Who's doing this?'

The soldiers advance through the mist; a group of Japanese soldiers is waiting. Attack. The Americans overrun a camp of Japanese soldiers, who are caught by surprise and unarmed. Some Japanese are taken prisoner, others killed. We apparently even see one American kill another in the confusion. After the fighting, Witt's inner voice says, 'This great evil. Who's doing this? Who's killing us?'

Witt shakes hands with a Japanese soldier, who looks quite like him, to comfort him. 'Does our ruin benefit the Earth?'

III. AFTER THE FIGHTING

23. Dale and the Japanese soldier

Dale speaks cruelly to one of the Japanese prisoners, who does not understand him, but repeats a phrase that is incomprehensible to the American soldier: '*Kisamawa shinundayo*'. Dale tells him he will die, devoured by scavenging birds, then turns his attention to the body of a Japanese soldier, whose gold teeth he wants to extract.

24. Witt remembers the earthly paradise

Soldiers refresh themselves in a river; Witt remembers the Melanesian village we saw at the beginning, and the earthly paradise. The beauty and peace of nature.

25. Staros relieved of his command

Tall tells Staros he is relieving him of his command – a decision he has taken with difficulty. He tells him he is 'too soft' and reminds him that nature is cruel. But at the same time, Tall does not want this to be a stain on Staros's career. He can be issued with a fake medical certificate for malaria. Tall tells Staros he will try to get him some medals in recognition of his wounds.

A congratulatory message to the troop from Tall is read by Welsh. 'Tomorrow … we're to be relieved. I've secured for the battalion a week's rest off the line.'

Tall alone. What is left of the Japanese camp is burned. A Buddha. Wooden wind-chimes.

27. The soldiers' joy
The soldiers go off on leave in a truck. They have food and drink (Witt's inner voice without his body: 'hours like months, days like years').

28. Staros says goodbye to his soldiers: 'You are my sons'
Staros says goodbye to his soldiers. Doll thanks him in the name of C Company for having protected them. The soldiers offer to intercede on his behalf. Staros refuses, says he is glad to be leaving, but that they have been like sons to him. Staros's inner voice, as he flies off in a plane: 'You are my sons, you live inside me now.'

29. Joy and suffering
Soldiers bathe, with joyful shouts.

Group scenes, soldiers fighting, accompanied by Doll's inner voice: 'War don't ennoble men; it turns 'em to dogs.'

Dale – the man with the gold teeth – alone, weeps in the rain as he remembers the incomprehensible words of the Japanese prisoner.

30. Bell thinks of his wife; Welsh and Storm
Bell walking alone, over which we hear the text of a love-letter to his wife: 'I wanna stay changeless for you.' Images of her (on a swing).

Dialogue between sergeants Storm and Welsh: the former feels he has lost all feeling, Welsh says he hasn't quite. Perhaps he was already 'frozen up' inside.

A bound crocodile is presented to some soldiers.

Bell to Fife (eating next to him): 'I haven't touched a woman.' Images of his wife.

31. Marty Bell's letter
Mail distribution. Bell receives and reads a letter. It is from his wife, read aloud by her voice. She has fallen in love with an Air Force captain: 'I want a divorce to marry him.' 'Oh my friend of these shining years. Help me leave you.' Images of this woman, gradually less visible: a mirror, then empty sheets. Bell is alone. His inner voice has fallen silent.

32. The Melanesian village: Witt cannot return to his earthly paradise

Jack Witt goes back to the Melanesian village. Sickness (malaria) is everywhere, the children are afraid of him, the men quarrel, a little girl scratches herself. We see human skulls (cannibalism?). Witt's interior monologue, accompanying flashback images of the happy times: 'We were a family. How'd it break up?'

33. Witt and the abandoned soldier

On his way back to camp, Witt meets a soldier who has been left alone at the roadside because he has been wounded in the knee. He is quietly

Bell's wife on a swing. Human skulls in a Melanesian village

waiting for more soldiers to come along and declines Witt's offer to help him walk.

34. Welsh and Witt in the ruined house: 'I still see a spark in you'

Witt returns to camp. Men talking around a table, wounded men on stretchers. Bell alone in the grass, silent.

Witt and Welsh talk in the ruined house of a former plantation. Witt: 'You ever get lonely?' Welsh: 'Only around people. You still believe in the beautiful light, do you?' Witt: 'I still see a spark in you.'

35. Meditation

Night. Welsh is walking among the resting or sleeping soldiers; a voice meditates (inner voice): at the sight of a dying bird some see 'unanswered pain', others 'feel the glory'. Image of Witt sleeping: 'Feels something smiling through him.'

IV. WITT'S SACRIFICE, THE SURVIVORS LEAVE
36. A reconnaissance mission

The soldiers, apparently on their way off the island, are walking along a shallow river. The line has been cut and the Japanese are not far away. A sergeant sends Fife and the very young Coombs on reconnaissance. Witt offers to go with them.

Witt helps Coombs

37. Witt saves two comrades and chooses to remain

The American soldiers see a Japanese troop in helmets camouflaged with leaves. Shooting. Coombs is wounded. Witt tells Fife to go back and warn the group of the battalion's presence, tells the boy who is wounded and possibly dying to go down the river. Alone, he distracts the attention of the Japanese.

The troop of soldiers realises that Witt has sacrificed himself to enable them to escape the Japanese.

38. Witt's death

After running through the forest, Witt is surrounded by the Japanese in a clearing. One Japanese soldier says something to him that he does not understand. He raises his gun and falls under a hail of bullets.

The sun appears, as though through a breach opened by the shots. Image of Melanesian children swimming, accompanied by Witt, who is smiling.

A sublime tree, the tree of the beginning.

39. Welsh alone

At Witt's graveside, the soldiers and silent Welsh, on the verge of tears (inner voice: 'Where is your spark now?').

Welsh listens as a new captain, Bosche, makes a speech to the soldiers. Welsh's interior monologue: 'Everything a lie.' 'Make an island for himself.' 'You're in a box. A moving box.'

A young soldier: 'features of the same face?'

C Company passes military graves. Welsh makes a mental plea: 'A glance from your eyes and my life will be yours.' At that moment, a woman who is not looking at him, echoing the Melanesian of the beginning who did not look at the American soldiers, turns towards the troop.

40. Departure
In a vast landscape, the soldiers reach the beach. Side by side they climb into a landing craft en route to the ship that will take them away. Gaff talks about his youth, his experience of the worst. He is hoping that the best is yet to come. Interior monologue in Witt's voice: 'Where is it that we were together?' The voice moves among bodies whose voices we do not hear: 'Darkness and light, strife and love, are they workings of one mind? The features of the same face?' Doll alone, away from the others. Witt's voice, a prayer to his soul.

41. Images of the earthly paradise
No more voices, but three images: a river, a canoe carrying children sliding under trees; a pair of brilliantly coloured parrots; a small plant above the water, on the shore.

42. Final credits

Notes

1 'Entretien avec Terrence Malick' by Michel Ciment, *Positif* no. 170, June 1975.

2 A restraint he also shows in the representation of sexuality and nudity, even when the situation would seem to involve it (Bell and his wife together in *The Thin Red Line*).

3 Pierre de Cabissole, *La Bible dans l'oeuvre de Terrence Malick* (Paris: Sorbonne Nouvelle, 2003), p. 156.

4 A phrase echoed by Witt in what is perhaps the film's only 'psittacism'.

5 Humankind at war like an anthill scattered by the urine of a man pissing on it is the simple, irrefutable metaphor shown at the beginning of Sergio Leone's *Duck You Sucker* (1972), about the American Civil War. War as a silent chaos stripped of meaning or voices, over which only music reigns, is also a famous cinema image, magnified by Kurosawa in *Ran* (1985), but from which *The Thin Red Line* also distances itself. In Malick's film, the words never give up.

6 We should note that Malick does not use the classic point-of-view shot of the 'scene seen from a distance through binoculars', which would allow the viewer a moment's identification with a view from outside the action. We always stay with and among the soldiers. Similarly, in the rare shots external to this action that tell us that at the top there is a machine gun firing through a slit, we are not shown the Americans in their sights, identifying the aim of the camera with that of the weapon, as Kubrick does in *Full Metal Jacket* (1987).

7 Cabissole, *La Bible*, p. 156

8 Clearly, this is not to make Malick into a creationist! Nor even to give his film a creationist meaning. It is just that the theory of evolution may not give us any answer to the division caused in creation by the appearance of language. Let us repeat that one of the meanings of *The Thin Red Line* is that language never gives up.

9 A forerunner of the well-known Steadicam, much discussed in relation to Kubrick's use of it in *The Shining* (1980). However, we should note that Kubrick, like John Boorman before him in *Exorcist II: The Heretic* (1977), uses this means of carrying the camera to follow characters along narrow corridors and passages, whereas from the outset, Malick uses it to move the camera around the characters in the open air, in an unenclosed setting.

10 *David Lynch*, 2nd edn (London: BFI Publishing, 2005).

11 Paris: Cahiers du Cinéma, 2003.

12 According to symbolism current in the cinema, soldiers returning home travel from right to left, whereas the attack on hill 210 was mainly undertaken from left to right.

Credits

The Thin Red Line

USA
1998

Directed by
Terrence Malick
Produced by
Robert Michael Geisler
John Roberdeau
Grant Hill
Screenplay by
Terrence Malick
Based upon the novel by
James Jones
Director of Photography
John Toll
Edited by
Billy Weber
Leslie Jones
Saar Klein
Production Designer
Jack Fisk
Music by
Hans Zimmer

©20th Century-Fox Film
Corporation
Production Companies
Fox 2000 Pictures presents
from Phoenix Pictures
in association with
George Stevens Jr
a Geisler-Roberdeau
production
Executive Producer
George Stevens Jr
Associate Producers
Michael Stevens,
Sheila Davis Lawrence
US Production Supervisor
Rosanna Sun
Production Accountant
Robert Threadgold
**Solomon Islands/
Guadalcanal Unit
Production Accountant**
Kevin Plummer
1st Assistant Accountant
Angela Kenny
**LA Post-production Units
1st Assistant Accountant**
Joanie Spates

2nd Assistant Accountant
Fiona Landreth
Payroll Accountant
Kylie Wilkie-Smith
Extras Payroll Accountant
Joanne Newell
Accounts Assistant
John Bailey
US Accounting Services
Owen & DeSalvo Company
**Post-production
Accountant**
Joanie Wooten-Spates-Ahuna
Production Co-ordinator
Serena Gattuso
2nd Unit Co-ordinator
Julie Sims
**Assistant Production
Co-ordinator**
Debbie Atkins
Production Manager
Vicki Popplewell
**Solomon Islands/
Guadalcanal Unit
Production Manager**
Amanda Crittenden
Unit Production Manager
Grant Hill
Unit Manager
Dick Beckett
2nd Unit Unit Manager
Paul Messer
**Solomon Islands/
Guadalcanal Unit Unit
Manager**
Simon Lucas
Assistant Unit Manager
Simon Lucas
Location Manager
Murray Boyd
2nd Unit Location Manager
Todd Fellman
**Solomon Islands/
Guadalcanal Unit Location
Manager**
Robin Clifton
**LA Post-production Units
Location Manager**
Ken Haber
**Los Angeles Liaison/
Assistant to Mr Hill**
Matt Bilski

**Solomon Islands/
Guadalcanal Unit Local
Liaison**
Victor Totu
Location Scout
Karen Jones
Camp Manager
Meghan Bailey
Post-production Supervisor
Jessica Alan
Post-production Assistant
Tim Floreen
Production Secretary
Kerry Mulgrew
Assistants to Mr Malick
Sandy Hastings
Aimee Nicholson
Assistant to Mr Stevens
Dottie McCarthy
**Assistants to
Geisler-Roberdeau**
Claudia Myers
Kim M. Rabsatt
**Assistant to Mr Hill
(Australia)**
Leoni Strickland
**LA Post-production Units
Assistant to Mr Travolta**
Susan Such
**Production Assistant/
Script Co-ordinator**
Emily Saunders
Production Assistant
Jenny Norman
**LA Post-production Units
Production Assistants**
Kayce Brown
Joel Elliott
Mike Estrella
Brandon Lambdin
Dan Mailley
Tim Pickering
Toddy E. Walters
**Solomon Islands/
Guadalcanal Unit
Production Office Assistant**
Sophia Chottu
Set Production Assistants
Hannah Browne
Giovanni Pacialeo
**2nd Unit Set Production
Assistant**
Rudy Joffroy

Production Runners
Colin Heidke
Jeffrey Heidke
Kent Sherlock
Los Angeles Production Runner
Paul Littleton
Solomon Islands/ Guadalcanal Unit Production Runners
Douglas Chottu
James Chottu
Unit Assistants
Sandra Bostok
Fred Braat
Camilla Crossing
Kim Gladman
Steve Hawker
Karl Hewitson
Jim Hewitson
Jody Hewitson
Katrina Mills
Richard Miller
Garry O'Conner
Ron Wyndam
2nd Unit Unit Assistant
Toshi
Solomon Islands/ Guadalcanal Unit Unit Assistant
Brendon Atong
2nd Unit Director
Gary Capo
First Assistant Director
Skip Cosper
Second Assistant Directors
Karen Estelle Collins
Simon Warnock
Second Second Assistant Director
Jennifer Leacey
Third Assistant Director
Andrew Power
2nd Unit First Assistant Director
Toby Pease
2nd Unit Second Assistant Director
Keri Bruno
2nd Unit Third Assistant Director
Tom Read
LA Post-production Units First Assistant Directors
L. Dean Jones
Sean Hobin

LA Post-production Units Second Second Assistant Director
Lisa Brookes
Script Supervisor
Chrissy O'Connell
2nd Unit Script Supervisor
Pam Willis
Solomon Islands/ Guadalcanal Unit Continuity
Alexandra W.-B. Malick
Continuity Assistant
Annie Renehan
Casting by
Dianne Crittenden
Casting Associate
Barbara Collins
Casting Agent (Japan)
M.M.I. International & Associates
Casting Agent (Australia)
Alison Barrett Casting
Regional Casting Agents
Jo Doster
Jo Edna Boldin
Extras Casting Agent (Australia)
Judith Cruden
Japanese Extras Co-ordinator
Martin Belson
Assistant Extras Co-ordinator
Ranjini Rusch
Solomon Islands/ Guadalcanal Unit Extras Casting
Louise Mitchell
ADR Voice Casting
L.A. MadDogs
Solomon Islands 2nd Unit Cameraman
Reuben Aaronson
Camera Operator/ Steadicam Operator
Brad Shield
2nd Unit Camera Operator
Leigh MacKenzie
LA Post-production Units Camera Operators
Steve Campanelli
Mike Thomas
First Assistant Camera/Focus Pullers
Darrin Keough
Brett Matthew
Frank Hruby

2nd Unit Focus Pullers
Adam Hammon
John Wareham
LA Post-production Units First Assistant Camera
Tony Rivetti
Chad Rivetti
Patty Van Over
Second Assistant Camera/Clapper Loaders
Louise William
Michi Marosszeky
Dugal Campbell
Rachel Fairfax
2nd Unit Second Assistant Camera/Clapper Loader
Matt Toll
Solomon Islands 2nd Unit Camera Assistants
Richard Confalone
Mauricio Gutierrez
LA Post-production Units Second Assistant Camera
Megan Forst
Frank Parrish
Chris Toll
LA Post-production Units Loader
Sal Alvarez
Key Grip
David Nichols
2nd Unit Key Grip
Toby Copping
LA Post-production Units Key Grips
Paul Borchard
Herb Ault
Dolly Grip
Mick Vivien
LA Post-production Units Best Boy Grips
Jerry Deat
Dustin Ault
Libra Head Technician
Tim Cousins
LA Post-production Units Libra Head Technician
Nick Phillips
Grips
Jorge Escanuela
Greg Tidman
2nd Unit Grips
Matt Copping
Dave Hansen
Aaron Walker

LA Post-production Units
Grips
Eugene Bertschneider
Ron Nichols
Don Padilla
Harold Rabuse
Kyle Carden
Doug Cowden
Dave Morriso
Mark Pickens
Walter Royle
Dan Speiser
Grip Assistants
Simon Boag
Mal Booth
David Connell
Akela Crane Technicians
Michael Gough
Mark Willard
Akela Crane Provided by
Fluid Images, Inc
Scaffolder
Simon Ambrose
Scaffolding Assistant
Mick Casey
Gaffer
Mick Morris
2nd Unit Gaffer
Brett Jarman
LA Post-production Units
Gaffers
Randy Woodside
Jim Boyle
Best Boy Electric
Gary Hill
LA Post-production Units
Best Boy Electrics
Chris Napolitano
Darrin Porter
Electricians
Paul Cumming
Stephen Gray
Miles Jones
2nd Unit Electrician
Marcus Watson
LA Post-production Units
Electrics
Jerry Woodside
Sean Smith
Larry J. Richardson
Marc Shultz
Robert White
Still Photographer
Merie Wallace
Visual Effects by
Animal Logic

Visual Effects Supervisor
Chris Godfrey
Visual Effects Producer
Fiona Chilton
Visual Effects Designer
Simon Whiteley
Senior Digital Compositors
Kirsty Millar
John Breslin
Justin Bromley
Digital Compositor
Robin Cave
Pre-visualization
Compositor
Grant Everett
3D Animator
Ian Brown
System Administrator
Glen Sharah
Digital Film Services by
Cinesite
Special Effects
Co-ordinator
Brian Cox
Senior Special Effects
Technician
David Hardie
Special Effects Technicians
Patrick Carmiggelt
Paul Gorrie
Pauline Grebert
John Neal
Peter Parry
Albert Payne
Pieter Plooy
Walter van Veenendaal
Special Effects Assistant
Katherine Gamble
Model Makers
Mark Powell
Gary Sherline
Trevor Smith
Dallas Wilson
Graphic Artist
Mandy Willaton
Graphic Artist Assistant
Matthew Willaton
Film Editor
Clarinda Wong
Assistant Editors
Charles Bunn
Laura Behary
Mark Ellis
Jenny Hicks
Alicia Gleeson
Avid Assistant
Derek McCants

Avid Technical Support
Warren Barnhart
Avid Film Composers
Provided by
Frameworks & Eagle Eye
Digital Film
Art Director
Ian Gracie
Assistant Art Director
Jeff Thorp
Solomon Islands 2nd Unit
Assistant Art Director
Nicholas Brunner
Art Department
Co-ordinator
Jenny O'Connell
Assistant to Art Department
Co-ordinator
Mick Plummer
Art Department Assistants
Steve Davey
Patrick Moyles
Barry Thompson
Sam Ward
Solomon
Islands/Guadalcanal Unit
Art Department Assistants
Peter Besi
Michael Selea
Beato Varahana
Art Department Runners
Michael Hunt
Joanna Robinson
Art Department Runner
(Sydney)
Andy Robillard
Set Decorators
Richard Hobbs
Suza Maybury
LA Post-production Units
Set Decorator
Rosemary Brandenburg
Set Dresser
Daryl Porter
Scenic Artist
Peter Collias
Storyboard Artists
Mark Lambert Bristol
David Russell
LA Post-production Units
Storyboard Artists
Jay Gibson
Greg Pallini
Sculptor
Guideo Helmstetter

LA Post-production Units
Swing
Chris Kennedy
Tom Traugott
Property Master
Richie Dehne
2nd Unit Stand-by Property
Master
James Cox
LA Post-production Units
Property Masters
Victor Petrotta Jr
Bill Petrotta
LA Post-production Units
Assistant Property Masters
Victor Petrotta III
Michael R. Gannon
Stand-by Props
Robert Moxham
Assistant Stand-by Props
Peter Kodicek
Katie Sharrock
Props Buyers/
Set Dressers
Rolland Pike
Bev Dunn
Sophie Tarney
Brock Sykes
Lead Prop Maker
Dick Weight
Construction Manager
Greg Hajdu
Construction Foreman
Mark Jones
Leading Hands
Eugene Land
Wayne Porter
Steel Workers
Peter Exton
Stewart Lewis
Rod Nash
Carpenters
Sean Ahern
Anthony Giltrap
Mark Laity
Steve Leslie
Ron Martin
Tony Peters
Dave Rogers
Trade Assistants
Ben Foley
Mick Owen
Kevin Ryan
LA Post-production Units
Paint Foreman
Michael Parent

Set Painters
Andy Robinson
Nicholas Walker
LA Post-production Units
Painters
Kelly Deco
Scott B. Dietz
Christian Klump
Set Finishers
Alan Brown
Gary Grimes
Brush Hand
Glenn Neal
Construction Assistants
Ron Dean
Flemming Olsson
Construction Runner
Bill Goodes
Greens Supervisor
Gregg Thomas
Stand-by Greens
Shane Bennett
Greensmen
Peter Johnston
Matt Jordin
Ron Wallekers
Trent Williamson
Costume Designer
Margot Wilson
Costume Supervisor
Kerry Thompson
Los Angeles Costumer
Liaison
Nanrose Buchman
LA Post-production Units
Costumers
Harold Crawford
Jimmy Cullen
Key Stand-by Costumer
Julie Barton
Stand-by Costumers
Michael Davies
Kate Green
Peter O'Halloran
2nd Unit Stand-by
Costumer
Mary-Lou Da Roza
Props Costumers
Ken Barnett
Chantelle Cordey
Costume Assistants
Lisa Collins
Tarnie Wilkie Smith
Cheryl Tootell
Goy Siriporn Wongwatawat

LA Post-production Units
Costume/Webbing
Assistants
Jeff Buhler
Talia Jones
Costumer Construction
Sandi Cichello
Military Webbing
Supervisor
Phil Eagles
Military Webbing Stand-by
Costumers
Angi Velickovic
Matthew Kinman
Military Webbing
Assistants
Clare Budd
David Cartmill
Mitch Morris
Sally Wilson
Military Webbing Adviser
Jim Dedman
Make-up/Hair Designer
Viv Mepham
Make-up
Artists/Hairdressers
Angela Conte
Toni French
Joan Petch
Chiara Tripodi
Additional Make-up/Hair
Rebecca Smith
Tracey Garner
Sarah Urquhart
LA Post-production Units
Additional Make-up/Hair
Michelle Burke-Winter
Sue Kalinowski
2nd Unit Stand-by
Make-up/Hair
Deb Lester
Make-up/Hair Assistant
Erica Wells
LA Post-production Units
Make-up/Hair Assistant
John Bird
Titles and Opticals
Consultant
Rob Yamamoto
Titles by
Scarlet Letters
End Credits by
Cinema Research Corporation
Opticals
Pat Doyle
Pacific Title/Mirage

Colour Timer
David Orr
Film Provided by
Kodak Australasia, P/L
Dailies Telecine by
Video 8
Additional Music by
John Powell
Francesco Lupica
Cosmic Beam Experience
Beam Supplemented by
Jeff Rona
Conductor
Gavin Greenaway
Orchestrators
Bruce Fowler
Yvonne S. Moriarty
**Additional Music
Arrangements by**
Klaus Badelt
Music Supervisor
Rosanna Sun
Music Co-ordinator
Maggie Rodford/Air-Edel
Associates Ltd
Composer Wrangler
Moanike'ala Nakamoto
Assistants to Mr Zimmer
Justin Burnett
Gregory Scott Newman
Music Editors
Lee Scott
Adam Smalley
Assistant Music Editor
Scott Rouse
Music Contractors
Sandy De Crescent
David Low
Music Copyist
Jo Ann Kane Music Service
**Music Production Services
by**
Media Ventures, Santa Monica
**Media Ventures Studio
Manager**
Tom Broderick
**Media Ventures
Engineering Team**
Gregg Silk
Slamm Andrews
Kevin Globerman
Bruno Roussel
Music Scoring Mixer
Alan Meyerson
Scoring Recordist
John Rodd

Scoring Stage Crew
Tom Stele
Damon Tedesco
Dennis Sager
Scoring Recorded at
Newman Scoring Stage,
20th Century-Fox
Technical Score Adviser
Marc Streitenfeld
Soundtrack
'Annum per annum' by Arvo
Pärt, performed by Andrew
Lucas, organ, at St Paul's
Cathedral, London (Courtesy
of ©Universal Editions, Wien &
Hyperion Records Ltd,
London, England © 1998);
'Requiem - In Paradisum' by
Gabriel Fauré, performed by
Orchestre de la Suisse
romande, Armin Jordan,
conductor (Courtesy of
Editions Hamelle, Paris &
©Erato Disques S.A. 1992);
'Sit Back and Relax'
by/performed by Francesco
Lupica, re-produced by Media
Ventures, Los Angeles
(Courtesy of Wonderment
Publishing Co. & Cosmic
Beam Records); 'The
Unanswered Question' by
Charles Ives, performed by The
Orchestra of St Luke's, John
Adams, conductor (Courtesy
of Peer International
Corporation & Nonesuch
Records by arrangement with
Warner Special Products); 'The
Prophecy from the Village of
Kremnus' by/performed/
produced by Arsenije
Jovanovic (Courtesy of
Arsenije Jovanovic & The
Adriatic Sound Factory)
Soundtrack Available on
RCA Victor
Sound Designers
John Fasal
Claude Letessier
Assistant Sound Designer
François Blaignan
Co-sound Supervisor
Robb Wilson
Sound Mixer
Paul 'Salty' Brincat

**LA Post-production Units
Additional Sound Mixer**
Susan Moore-Chong
Recordists
Robert Renga
Craig 'Pup' Heath
2nd Unit Sound Recordist
Greg Burgmann
Boom Person
Rod Conder
2nd Boom Person
Gary Dixon
**LA Post-production Units
Boom Operators**
Jeffrey Williams
Charles Payne
**Cable Person/Additional
Boom**
Steven King
Video Split Operator
Mark Holtermann
**2nd Unit Video Split
Operator**
Chris Healy
Re-recording Mixers
Andy Nelson
Anna Behlmer
Additional Mixer
Jim Bolt
Engineer
Denis St Amand
Re-recording Services by
20th Century-Fox Studios
Supervising Sound Editor
J. Paul Huntsman
Dialogue Editors
Patrick J. Foley
John F. Reynolds
Virginia Cook McGowan
Sound Effects Editors
Christopher S. Aud
John V. Bonds Jr
Jayme S. Parker
Andrew M. Sommers
Mark Mangino
Assistant Sound Editors
Jeff Cranford
David Werntz
Todd Harris
Sound Editorial by
Warner Bros. Post-Production
Sound
Negative Cutting by
The Conformist, Inc
ADR Supervisor
Hugh Waddell
ADR Recordist
Rick Canelli

ADR Mixer
Thomas J. O'Connell
ADR Editors
Lee Lamont
Karyn Foster
Conforming Editor
Hugo Weng
Voice-over Supervisor
James Simcik
Foley Supervisor
Jeffrey Rosen
Foley Artists
John B. Roesch
Hilda Hodges
Foley Recordist
Carolyn Tapp
Foley Mixer
Mary Jo Lang
Foley Editor
David Horton Jr
Dialect Coach
Lilene Mansell
Japanese Advisers
Shin Watarai
Tomo Miyaguchi
Key Military Adviser
Mike Stokey
Assistant Military Advisers
Dale Dye
Pablo Espinosa
Royce Perkins
Reuben Romo
Raleigh Wilson
Stunt Co-ordinator
Glenn Boswell
LA Post-production Units
Stunt Co-ordinator
Raleigh Wilson
Stunt Co-ordinator's
Assistant
Zelie Thompson
Stunt Performers
Shea Adams
Dean Bennett
Richard Boue
Bob Bowles
Mick Corrigan
Mitch Deans
Paul Doyle
Mark Eady
Nash Edgerton
Johnny Hallyday
Nigel Harbach
Steve Harman
Lou Horvath
Phil Meacham
Chris Mitchell
Darren Mitchell

Mick Van Moorsel
Scott O'Donnell
Brett Praed
Greg Robinson
Glenn Suter
Darko Tuskan
David Woodley
Additional Stunt
Performers
Bob Arnold
Scott Blackwood
Joey Box
Chris Branham
Leon Delaney
Dennis Fitzgerald
Tanner Gill
Gary Guercio
Toby Holguin
Jessie Johnson
Johnny Martin
Brian Moore
James Paul Morse
Vladimir Orlov
Mike Owen
Jim Palmer
Mark Riccardi
Felipe Savahge
Mike Smith
Greg Smrz
Mark Stefanich
Key Armourer
John Bowring
Armourers
Peter Cogar
Amanda Kirby
Allen Mowbray
Bob Parsons
Scott Warwick
Armourer Assistants
Jeffrey Gribble
Miles Jackson
Phillip Young
Armoury Workshop
Assistants
Mark Buttsworth
Donovan Norguard
Aircraft Co-ordinator
Bruce Simpson
Pilots
Guy Bourke
John Curtis
Doug Haywood
Owen O'Malley
John Rayner
Ray Seaver
Ralph Simpson
Marine Co-ordinator
Lance Julian

Assistant Marine
Co-ordinators
Harry L.H. Julian Sr
Nick Spetsiotis
Marine Engineers
Danny Dade
Joe Donaldson
Gert Jacoby
Marine Boat Captains
Julian Barton
Rhodes Barton
Brett Bastow
Brian Bradley
Rob Collins
Barry Collins
Eugene L. Geyl
Daniel Keith Hobbs
Simon Primrose
Fleur Quinn
Jason Shearer
LA Post-production Units
Boat Captains
Daniel Bailey
Ron Byrd
Mark Hornton
Al Perry
Danny Trefts
Rob Wong
LA Post-production Units
Boat Winchmen
Mike Douglas
Rick Hicks
Shipwright
Carl Raab
Assistant Engineer
Roy McGuffie
LA Post-production Units
Dock Master
Mike George
LA Post-production Units
Safety Divers/Deckhands
Greg Tash
Daniel Hart
Tom Wyatt
Transportation
Co-ordinator
John Suhr
LA Post-production Units
Transportation
Co-ordinators
Roger Hanna
Kevin Scott
Assistant Transportation
Co-ordinators
Philip Meurant
Russell Boyd

LA Post-production Units
Transportation Captain
Howard Bachrach
Action Vehicle Co-ordinator
Tim Parry
On-set Vehicle
Co-ordinator
Paul Naylor
Action Vehicle Assistant
Reginald Marteene
Drivers (Australia)
Kerry Bushnell
Alan Cooke
Rodney Dack
Dave Heazlewood
Benjamin Lindell
Sally-Ann Louisson
Alan MacClure
Rick MacClure
Nick Stewart
Kevin Urquhart
Hans Van Beuge
Gerrit Van Dijk
Solomon Islands/
Guadalcanal Unit Drivers
(Solomon Islands)
Sam Collins
Albert Cooke
Ben Jim
Leslie Kili
Stephen Leong
Fabby La
Isaac Onio
Ninamo Otuano
Kevin Pitanoe
Jenny Polyn
Abraham Pwaholo
Vivienne Sahedy
Barnabus Samani
Norman Samson
Daisy Ta'ake
Lynette Tokatake
Travel/Accommodations
Co-ordinator
Melaini Lewis
Freight Co-ordinator
Mike Harper
Freight Assistant
David Clark
Freight Runner
Richard McCarthy
Safety Officer
Claude Lambert
2nd Unit Safety Officer
Brian Ellison
Assistant Safety Officer
Chris Mitchell

Medical Staff
Ron Houghton
Jacquie Robertson
Rachel Vogelpoel
Solomon Islands/
Guadalcanal Unit Medical
Officer
L. Douglas Fenton
LA Post-production Units
Medical Co-ordinator
L. Douglas Fenton
2nd Unit Unit Nurse
Evelyn Driver
LA Post-production Units
First Aid Nurses
Alex Barynoya
Gloria Fujita
Caterer
Kerry Fetzer
Solomon Islands/
Guadalcanal Unit Caterer
Tony Wilxox
Catering Assistants
Irene Augerinos
Michael Dalmas
Guy Firth
Chris Herron
Ian Hunter
Christobel Jefferies
Reza Mokhtar
Jenny Wilson
LA Post-production Units
Catering/Craft Service
DeLuxe Catering
Rick Brainin Catering
David Kasubowski
Peter Evangelatos
Dailies Projectionist
Victor Roger Monk
Solomon Islands/
Guadalcanal Unit Local
Police/Security
Simon Houma
Moses Lakwolly
Andrew Toritarau
Solomon Islands 2nd Unit
Anthropologist
Christine Jourdan
LA Post-production Units
Teacher
L. Richard Wickland
Unit Publicist
Fiona Searson/DDA Public
Relations
US Publicist
Pat Kingsley/PMK Public
Relations

The Director and Producers
Wish to Thank the
Following for Their
Assistance
Penny Allen, Daniel Aukin,
Henry Bamberger, Walter H.
Bradford, Ray Elliott, Lukas
Haas, Eryna Heisler, Kevin
Heisler, Gloria Jones, Jamie
Jones, Kaylie Jones, Randall
Duk Kim, Darrell Kirkland,
Harold Lee, Donal Logue,
Francine Maisler, John
McNees, Barry McPaul, Robert
Miranda, Viggo Mortensen,
Amanda Nelligan, Lindy
Neuhaus, David Paschall,
Jason Patric, Barry Paterson,
Jace Phillips, David Pratt, John
Price, Bill Pullman, Jason
Rabe, Robert L. Rosen, Mickey
Rourke, Martin Sheen, Thomas
Sumners, Billy Bob Thornton,
Carey Phillips Turner, Harley
Williams, John Womack Jr,
Brother Zephaniah, Tim
Zinnemann, The Community of
Port Douglas, Queensland,
Australia; The People of the
Solomon Islands; The Choir of
All Saints, Honiara; The
Melanesian Brotherhood; The
Staff and Crew of *The Lane*
Victory; The City of San Pedro,
CA; Guadalcanal Veterans
Association; Aus FILM; The
Australian Pacific Film and
Television Commission
(PFTC); Film Freight
International; Travel Too;
Queensland Ambulance
Service, FNQ, Cairns, Australia

Cast
Sean Penn
First Sergeant Edward Welsh
Adrien Brody
Corporal Geoffrey Fife
Jim Caviezel
Private Bob Witt
Ben Chaplin
Private John 'Jack' Bell
George Clooney
Captain Charles Bosche
John Cusack
Captain John Gaff
Woody Harrelson
Sergeant Keck

Elias Koteas
Captain James 'Bugger'
Staros
Jared Leto
Second Lieutenant William
Whyte
Dash Mihok
Private First Class Don Doll
Tim Blake Nelson
Private Tills
Nick Nolte
Lieutenant Colonel Gordon Tall
John C. Reilly
Sergeant Storm
Larry Romano
Private Mazzi
John Savage
Sergeant McCron
John Travolta
Brigadier General Quintard
Arie Verveen
Private First Class Charlie Dale
Kirk Acevedo
Private Alfred Tella
Penny Allen
Witt's mother
Benjamin
Melanesian villager
Simon Billig
Lieutenant Colonel Billig
Mark Boone Junior
Private Peale
Norman Patrick Brown
Private Henry
Jarrod Dean
Corporal Thorne
Matt Doran
Private Coombs
Travis Fine
Private Weld
Paul Gleeson
First Lieutenant George Band
David Harrod
Corporal Queen
Don Harvey
Sergeant Becker
Kengo Hasuo
Japanese prisoner
Ben Hines
assistant pilot
Danny Hoch
Private Carni
Robert Roy Hofmo
Private Sico
Jack
Melanesian man walking
Tom Jane
Private Ash

Jimmy
Melanesian villager
Polyn Leona
Melanesian woman with child
Simon Lyndon
medic 2
Gordon MacDonald
Private First Class Earl
Kazuki Maehara
Japanese private 1
Marina Malota
Marina
Michael McGrady
Private Floyd
Ken Mitsuishi
Japanese officer 1
Ryushi Mizukami
Japanese private 4
Larry Neuhaus
crewman
Taiju Okayasu
Japanese private 6
Takamitsu Okubo
Japanese soldier
Miranda Otto
Marty Bell
Kazuyoshi Sakai
Japanese prisoner 2
Masayuki Shida
Japanese officer 2
John Dee Smith
Private Edward B. Train
Stephen Spacek
Corporal Jenks
Nick Stahl
Private First Class Bead
Hiroya Sugisaki
Japanese private 7
Kouji Suzuki
Japanese private 3
Tomohiro Tanji
Japanese private 2
Minoru Toyoshima
Japanese sergeant
Terutake Tsuji
Japanese private 5
Steven Vidler
2nd Lieutenant Albert Gore
Vincent
Melanesian guide
Todd Wallace
pilot
Will Wallace
Private Hoke
Joe Watanabe
Japanese officer 3
Simon Westaway
Stack, first scout

Dan Wyllie
medic 1
Yasuomi Yoshino
young Japanese
John Augwata
Joshua Augwata
John Bakotee
Immanuel Dato
Michael Iha
Emmunual Konai
Stephen Konai
Peter Morosiro
Amos Niuga
Jennifer Siugali
Carlos Tome
Selina Tome
Melanesian extras

[*uncredited*]
Donal Logue
Marl
Randall Duk Kim
Nisei interpreter
Clark McCutchen
soldier
Felix Williamson
Private Drake
Jace Phillips
S-1
David Paschall
general
Charlie Beattie
Kick Gurry
Darrin Klimek

15,353 feet
170 minutes 35 seconds

Dolby Digital
Colour by
Atlab
Prints by
Technicolor
2.35:1 [Panavision]
MPAA: 36486

Filmed on Location in
Queensland, Australia;
Guadalcanal, The Solomon
Islands and San Pedro,
California

Credits compiled by Markku
Salmi

The Thin Red Line is available
on DVD from 20th Century-Fox
Home Entertainment

Also Published

Amores Perros
Paul Julian Smith (2003)

L'Argent
Kent Jones (1999)

Blade Runner
Scott Bukatman (1997)

Blue Velvet
Michael Atkinson (1997)

Caravaggio
Leo Bersani & Ulysse Dutoit (1999)

A City of Sadness
Bérénice Reynaud (2002)

Crash
Iain Sinclair (1999)

The Crying Game
Jane Giles (1997)

Dead Man
Jonathan Rosenbaum (2000)

Dilwale Dulhaniya Le Jayenge
Anupama Chopra (2002)

Don't Look Now
Mark Sanderson (1996)

Do the Right Thing
Ed Guerrero (2001)

Easy Rider
Lee Hill (1996)

The Exorcist
Mark Kermode (1997, 2nd edn 1998, rev. 2nd edn 2003)

Eyes Wide Shut
Michel Chion (2002)

Groundhog Day
Ryan Gilbey (2004)

Heat
Nick James (2002)

The Idiots
John Rockwell (2003)

Independence Day
Michael Rogin (1998)

Jaws
Antonia Quirke (2002)

L.A. Confidential
Manohla Dargis (2003)

Last Tango in Paris
David Thompson (1998)

Nosferatu – Phantom der Nacht
S.S. Prawer (2004)

Once Upon a Time in America
Adrian Martin (1998)

Pulp Fiction
Dana Polan (2000)

The Right Stuff
Tom Charity (1997)

Saló or The 120 Days of Sodom
Gary Indiana (2000)

Seven
Richard Dyer (1999)

The Shawshank Redemption
Mark Kermode (2003)

The Silence of the Lambs
Yvonne Tasker (2002)

The Terminator
Sean French (1996)

Thelma & Louise
Marita Sturken (2000)

The Thing
Anne Billson (1997)

The 'Three Colours' Trilogy
Geoff Andrew (1998)

Titanic
David M. Lubin (1999)

Trainspotting
Murray Smith (2002)

Unforgiven
Edward Buscombe (2004)

The Usual Suspects
Ernest Larsen (2002)

The Wings of the Dove
Robin Wood (1999)

Withnail & I
Kevin Jackson (2004)

Women on the Verge of a Nervous Breakdown
Peter William Evans (1996)

WR – Mysteries of the Organism
Raymond Durgnat (1999)